Dissenting

SELECTED
ESSAYS

Opinions

Page Smith

North Point Press
San Francisco
1984

Library of Congress Catalogue Card Number:83–063125
ISBN:0–86547–154–1

Grateful acknowledgment is made to the following periodicals, in which some of these essays appeared in slightly different form: *William and Mary Quarterly* ("Anxiety and Despair in American History"), *New Mexico Quarterly* ("Russell Kirk and the New Conservatism"), *Los Angeles Times* ("The Revolt of the Radical Realists," "The Lost Art of Declamation," "Confessions of a Twelve O'Clock Scholar," "The Vanishing Gentleman," "Nurses and Nannies," "Home, Sweet Home," "Fidelity," "The Original Fourth of July Parade," "The Founders and the Court," "Ford's Pardon of Nixon," "Civilization: It's the Little Things That Count," "Decisions, Decisions! They're Driving Us Daft," and "Samuel Eliot Morison, 1887–1976"), *The Journal of Religion* ("Wyndham Lewis's *America and Cosmic Man*), *Historical Reflections* ("From Masses to Peoplehood"), *Education Research Bulletin* ("The Sins of Higher Education"), *Halcyon: A Journal of the Humanities* ("The Inhuman Humanities"), *Journal of Higher Education* ("Human Time and the College Student"), *Learning* ("Students Don't 'Study' History—They Are History"), Research Center for Nonviolence *Newsletter* ("The New Abolitionism"), and *News and Notes of the UCSC Farm and Garden* ("In Memoriam: Alan Chadwick"). "The Universal Curriculum" and "The William James Association Newsletter" were originally published by the William James Association. "God's Voice and the American Revolution" was published in *The Religious Origins of the American Revolution* and "Tenure: Pushing Back the Frontiers of Knowledge" appeared in *City on a Hill*.

For Paul Lee

Contents

Introduction

The process of assembling the material herein included has been unsettling if perhaps salutary. It has led me to reflect on the unaccountability of my life (and my intense enjoyment of it) as well as my manifold debts to others both for the ideas that have dominated my life and for the generosity of what I must call for want of a better phrase their spiritual gifts. This is particularly true of my family, immediate and intermediate, and my teachers, a remarkably varied lot.

Some introductory comments might help readers place these pieces (and me) in context. Like the "short and simple annals of the poor," the essential facts of my biography can be briefly stated.

I was born at the Women's Hospital in Baltimore, Maryland, on September 6, 1917, the first of two male children of uneasily wedded upper middle (or lower upper) class parents. My mother was a gently nurtured Southern woman; my father was dedicated to the pursuit of happiness in the form of compliant females. My mother and father soon separated and later divorced, and my brother (five years younger than I) and mother and I went to live with my mother's parents in a large, ugly greenstone house with a mansard roof in the outer reaches of suburban Baltimore. It was a severe, old-fashioned Southern establishment with a large retinue of black servants—upstairs and downstairs maids, a waitress, a cook, a chauffeur, and a gardener (white). My grandfather was as silent as Calvin Coolidge, whom he admired even though Coolidge was a Republican (the last President of the United States worth his salt, in his view, was Grover Cleveland). My most persistent image of my banker grandfather is of him sitting behind a large mahogany desk in the central bank (he pioneered branch banks in Baltimore's "ethnic" neighborhoods) with the proud and confident look of de Lawd in *Green Pastures*, surveying what he had wrought and finding it good.

I was educated, in spite of my dogged resistance, at Gilman Country Day School, a bastion of the Baltimore establishment. My early ambition to be a "writer" stemmed from the intoxicating experience of discovering a responsive reader in Mr. Stendal, my fourth grade teacher. Mr. Stendal read aloud to the class an essay I had written on "The Servant Problem" as experienced in my grandparents' home. It dealt with the unhappy episode of a maid sent by an employment agency and discharged a few days later for impudence and inefficiency (mostly, I gathered, the former). She was a shapely mulatto woman in whom I had taken an immediate and precocious interest. The last sentence of the essay, which Mr. Stendal particularly commended, read: "The maid disappeared and so did the butter," a reference to the fact that the discharged maid had exacted a measure of revenge by carrying off several pounds of butter. Despite this modest literary triumph, my general academic performance was deplorable; I even repeated the fifth grade, an unprecedented disaster. This long and, for my mother at least, painful experience of my Gilman education was interrupted by a year at boarding school at Morristown, New Jersey, where it was hoped that, free of distractions, I would apply myself more rigorously to my studies (it was the common view that I was lazy rather than stupid). The boarding school interval was indeed educational though not, I fear, in the way that my mother had hoped. It gave me a certain insight into the mores of the Eastern upper class and, by extension, the British upper class and, perhaps more basically, into the hazards (or the opportunities, depending on your point of view) arising from institutionalizing young males.

Boarding school was followed by a dismal year at a military academy, apparently in the expectation that being in uniform would make me more disciplined in my study habits. Undisciplined as ever, I returned to Gilman as to home itself. I had put the school on its mettle. To get me through, one way or another, became a kind of faculty project. All that could be done by kindly and attentive teachers was done. Archie Hart taught me a little English (as much as I could be persuaded to absorb) and awakened and developed my interest in art. Herbert Pickett with his dry wit and dead pan made ancient history as current as the daily paper and far more interesting. Ed Russell got me, with infinite labor, through the opening paragraphs of *Caesar's Commentaries* (all I remember is that Gaul was divided into three parts), but he taught a number of nifty wrestling holds—the half nelson, sit-out, sit-through, arm roll, leg ride, etc.—that still serve me well in engagements with other historians, footpads, and members of my immediate family. But I will chronicle my academic failings more extensively later in this book. My wife has often charged me with excessive vanity in dwelling so long and lovingly on what someone with a better sense of proportion would, in her view, have passed over in silence.

At Dartmouth College I further benefited from my exposure to great teachers. Alan MacDonald was surely, in some happy platonic order, destined to be a teacher of freshman English. I shall never forget my initial outrage, followed by a shiver of pleasure, when he read the startling lines from T. S. Eliot's "The Love Song of J. Alfred Prufrock"—"Let us go then, you and I / When the evening is spread out against the sky / Like a patient etherized upon a table." For someone raised on the pleasant pieties of Longfellow and Whittier, it came as a decided shock to think that such an image might make a claim to be poetry. MacDonald read aloud from Hardy's *Tess* and suddenly Hardy was indispensable. He did the same with D. H. Lawrence and I fell in love with Lawrence at once; it proved a lifelong romance. I also fell in love with Alan MacDonald. With a classmate who shared my infatuation, we conspired to encounter him about the campus as though by chance. We lay in wait at the coffee shop he frequented. He asked us to join him at his table. He talked about the weather and the Boston Red Sox. We were entranced. Later my friend and I took a walk and made out that we had lost our way when we came to his house; we expressed surprise to discover that he lived there. We were in fact curious to see the woman fortunate enough to be married to a man so witty, brilliant, and handsome. Poor Mrs. MacDonald; we had a combination of Ingrid Bergman and Madame de Staël in mind. She looked like an ordinary faculty wife, the kind we saw around the campus every day. We were invited in to tea. The conversation was mundane; we departed bitterly disappointed in Mrs. MacDonald, feeling that Alan was more in need of our devotion than ever.

Not only was I an instant convert to "the new literature," I was, it turned out, equally susceptible to the "new politics." I left Baltimore for my freshman year a staunch Dixiecrat, that is to say, a Democrat who hated Franklin Roosevelt as the embodiment of evil. That was my grandfather's view, indeed the view of most members of my family (my mother was a mild dissenter) and virtually all of my friends and *their* families (I had two eccentric aunts who loved Mr. Roosevelt because he was such a gentleman). I came home the Christmas vacation of my freshman year with a copy of Karl Marx's *Das Kapital* in my suitcase. I was already a member of the minute campus chapter of the Young Communist League. It was all somewhat of a family scandal. An aunt began referring to me as "a pin-feather in the Left Wing." My grandfather's warning that college, especially a Yankee college, would prove highly demoralizing for a prospective banker seemed confirmed.

From Alan MacDonald, I graduated to Sidney Cox, friend of Robert Frost and teacher of creative writing. Cox, dry, homely, ineffably Yankee with a long mournful face and drawling New England accent, was the antithesis of Alan MacDonald, but my upper-class friends and counselors informed me that while Alan MacDonald's Lawrencian romanticism might be fine for naive freshmen, Sidney Cox was the real literary stuff. Budd Schulberg had been a student of Sidney's as had Raoul Denny, Bill Bronk, and a number of promising young literary lights. The trick was to attract Cox's favorable attention, typically in his writing class, and be invited to his Sunday evening literary gatherings, where poems, short stories, and essays were read and discussed. Another means of access was to have a well-established member of the group invite you to a kind of probationary evening. However I got in, those "evenings at Sidney's" became a central part of my college experience, more important to me than any class or combination of classes in my literature major. Feeling a little disloyal to Alan MacDonald, I settled happily into the Cox circle, which was as ideal for an upperclassman as MacDonald's had been for a freshman.

I don't believe you can teach writing and I doubt if Cox thought you could. I can't, in any event, recall anything that Sidney Cox taught me directly about writing, although he wrote a wonderful little book, an instant classic, called *Indirections, A Guide for People Who Want to Write*. But if you can't teach writing you can create what we call today "a supportive atmosphere," that is, you can encourage people to see and feel and think in ways that nourish life and thereby nourish writing, and this Sidney Cox did superbly. If, post-Cox, you never wrote a line, you were a wiser, more generous person for having known him. Or if you weren't it was your own fault. That has always remained for me the essence of teaching. I have never managed to do it so well as Sidney, God rest his soul, but at least he taught me what was required.

Finally, there was the remarkable man who more than anyone else (my mother and wife excepted) determined the shape and direction of my adult life. Eugen Rosenstock-Huessy, a refugee from Nazi Germany, had come to Dartmouth by way of Harvard a few years before I arrived there. He was a scholar in the great German tradition. More than that he was, in his words, "an impure thinker," that is to say, in no sense a traditional academic philosopher or, in fact, a traditional anything else. He was a thinker of startling power and originality, in my view an authentic genius of whom no age produces more than a handful. That he should appear on the campus of a provincial New England college with only the most modest pretensions to intellectual distinction (it did other equally important things very well as I hope I have made clear) was, in itself, a surprising consequence of these horrendous times. This is not the place for a resumé of his philosophical doctrines. It is perhaps sufficient to say that any errant scholars looking for the roots of my own views on history, and indeed life in general, can save themselves time and trouble by going directly to the work of Rosenstock-Huessy, or that rather small portion of it translated into English. Among other things, Rosenstock-Huessy inadvertently ended my relatively brief infatuation with Marxism (the German-Soviet Non-Aggression Pact of 1939 also helped substantially). While I can't recall Rosenstock-Huessy ever attacking Marxism per se, his view of man in history made Marxism seem superficial; valuable as a critical and analytical tool but entirely inadequate as a scheme for reordering the world.

In addition, Rosenstock-Huessy involved me, and a number of other recent Harvard and Dartmouth graduates, in one of the formative experiences of my life—Camp William James. He challenged us to make our educations stand for something by trying, with the support of Eleanor Roosevelt and her husband, to turn the emergency Depression-prompted Civilian Conservation Corps into a permanent work-service agency of the federal government. Camp William James, inspired by that American philosopher's essay, *A Moral Equivalent of War*, began in an abandoned CCC sidecamp in Sharon, Vermont, in the winter of 1940–41. I was the camp manager when I was drafted out of the camp into the Army of the United States in the spring of 1941. Like the thought of Rosenstock-Huessy, Camp William James is another story.

A few months after Pearl Harbor I went to Infantry Officer Training School at Fort Benning, Georgia. As soon as I had been commissioned a second lieutenant, I married an artist I had met during maneuvers in North Carolina a year earlier. After five years in the army, one of them as an instructor at the Infantry School and three as a company commander in the Tenth Mountain Division, I returned to Baltimore on convalescent leave and taught for a year at my alma mater, Gilman School; truly the return of the prodigal! I still wanted to be a writer, in practical terms a journalist/novelist, but some graduate study under the G.I. Bill of Rights seemed a reasonable interim step. I was accepted for graduate work in history at Harvard with a good deal of reluctance. The chairman of the history department informed me that I would find no extravagant Rosenstock-Huessy notions *there*. Harvard was a "trade school," not given to moony, Germanic speculations about the nature and destiny of man but to turning out academic historians intimately acquainted with footnotes and bibliographies (where, I wondered, did he think the American academic world had acquired its infatuation with the apparatus of scholarship?). In any event, through a series of coincidences as odd as those that had brought me into the orbit of a displaced German philosopher, I found myself the "reading assistant" of Samuel Eliot Morison, the last academic practitioner of the great nineteenth-century tradition of narrative history. When the chairman of the history department ratified my job as Morison's assistant, he observed cryptically that we would probably be "good for each other," which I later conjectured to mean that Morison's highly practical bent might temper my proclivity for vast generalizations about history; how he thought I might "be good for Morison," I never discerned. Perhaps he thought that I, as a conspicuously wounded war veteran still maneuvering about on crutches, might touch what was generally (and falsely) assumed to be Morison's flinty New England heart.

I can best suggest our relationship by noting that while Rosenstock-Huessy was the godfather of our older son, Morison was godfather of our younger. In any event I could not have been delivered into kinder or more generous hands. Perhaps the most important lesson I learned from Morison (who strengthened my inclination toward narrative history) was that being a professor was not wholly incompatible with living a civilized life. The notion had hardly occurred to me before, in part because I had never contemplated an academic career (small wonder considering my earlier scholastic performance), and in part because, at least at Harvard, it seemed so rare for faculty members to do so.

The fact was that I slipped into academic life as much by inertia as intent. A fellowship at the Institute of Early American History and Culture in Williamsburg, Virginia, designed to give recent Ph.D.'s in the field of colonial American history an opportunity to turn their dissertations into publishable books, opened up. Morison encouraged me to apply for it and supported my application. The fellowship was awarded jointly with the College of William and Mary and involved some teaching duties. We had been in Williamsburg only a year of the three-year fellowship period when an opening came in the history department at the University of California, Los Angeles. Again, Morison advised me to apply for the job; jobs were still hard to come by in the early 1950s. I was an extremely provincial Easterner who had never been west of western Maryland and the notion of going to a place as remote and bizarre as Los Angeles rather alarmed me (and dismayed my mother). It also meant abandoning whatever lingering notion I still harbored of becoming a journalist. But we went, my wife and three small children (our fourth was born in California). Going tentatively and with numerous reservations (we thought it would be "an interesting experience" for a year or so), we discovered to our surprise that we were "natural" Californians. That, too, is another story. After eleven years at UCLA, I was invited to come to Santa Cruz to organize and head (as "Provost") the first college of the new campus of the University of California at Santa Cruz. I thus had the unexpected opportunity to try to give effect to some of my criticisms of higher education, an irresistible prospect.

My nine years at Santa Cruz, five as Provost, four as Professor of Historical Studies, were totally absorbing. Perhaps the most rewarding aspect was that my wife, although she held no formal academic post, was a full and essential participant in developing the life of the college, particularly in the arts.

In 1973, I left the University in protest over the "termination," that is to say, firing, of my friend and colleague, Paul Lee, primarily on the ground that he had not published. Since I had long been a critic of the practice of requiring university teachers to publish something in order to be given tenure, that is, *de facto* life-long job security, it seemed to me appropriate to act in conformity with my convictions, especially in a case in which my own feelings were so directly involved.

Since then I have rusticated in the Santa Cruz mountains, sharing the modest duties as codirector of the William James Association with Paul Lee, writing, and tending various domestic creatures.

What all this has to do with the material in this volume will, hopefully, become evident to the patient reader. The book is, like Gaul, divided into three parts. Part One is composed of essays (some originally talks) having to do with my concerns as an historian. They extend from 1955 to 1983.

Part Two deals with my reflections on the general subject of education and covers a similar period of time. My concern with educational theory goes back, I suspect, to my elementary and secondary school days. There I expressed my critical response by the simple expedient of refusing to do the work required of me.

The third section is made up of occasional pieces, most of them written between 1954 and 1964 for the *Los Angeles Times*. Not only did they provide a modest augmentation to my modest salary as a junior faculty member, they allowed me the unexpected luxury of being a part-time journalist.

Reading the manuscript over, I was reminded of an episode that befell me many years ago. At a cocktail party prior to a dinner of the Brandeis Law Club in Philadelphia, I fell under the spell of a beautiful young woman who chose to confide in me the most intimate details of her romantic life (at least they seemed disarmingly intimate to me at that time and age). They centered on the fact that she was in love with and engaged in amours with a married man. I was, as always, replete with helpful advice, specifically that she should break off the illicit liaison at once, hoping dimly, I suspect, that I might become a replacement. Her manner, it must be said, encouraged such an expectation. I became so distracted by her enchanting smile (her distress had, if anything, heightened her beauty), her brilliant teeth, and her luminous eyes that I hardly followed the harrowing details of the relationship. When, at the end of the dinner, which featured a marvelous talk by the Chinese legal scholar and correspondent of Justice Holmes, Dr. Woo, I resumed what had by then become a rather ardent courtship, she dismissed me with a charming smile and a warm, lingering caress of my hand: "Page," she said, "I certainly have enjoyed talking with you. It's been real edificating." So much for my dreams of romance. It has been, I fear, my unhappy fate to be relentlessly "edificating," even when my intentions have been less honorable. There must, I have regretfully concluded, be something irredeemably avuncular about me, a dogmatism of uplift, an irrepressible preacherliness, that is doubtless an occupational hazard of the reform-minded.

Part One

History

Anxiety
1969 and Despair
in American History

Our times have been called the "Age of Anxiety" and though the point hardly needs special emphasis, I cannot resist belaboring it a little. In the *Medical Newsmagazine*, Volume 10, which I take to be a typical issue, there are 365 handsome pages with articles on fossils, archaic art, the story of the Nile, the life and work of Arnold Toynbee, the life and loves of Madame de Staël, plus a great many advertisements for the principal ills that beset the average American. These advertisements give a very curious and, I suspect, not wholly inaccurate profile of the state of our collective psyche. The picture is not a particularly cheering one. Almost 60 percent of the remedies offered are for nervous tension, 10 percent for the overweight, another 10 percent are for what has come to be known, rather starkly, as THE PILL. As we open the magazine we encounter Milpath, offered as "peace for the troubled gut: when your patients complain of belching, gnawing, burning, bloating, churning, tightening, quivering, rushing, loosening, rumbling, knotting, growling, gripping, gurgling, swelling, cramping especially in disorders accompanied by anxiety and tension." On the opposite page beside a very graphic picture of ringwormed toes, we have a column headed "The Adventure of Art." We then turn to Etrafon "when emotionally based complaints fit the symptom profile of depression . . . and insomnia predominates." On to Vistaril "in breadwinner's anxiety. . . . He is forty, but probably feels older. His income is average, but he thinks it inadequate." To Fiorinal "for tension headaches"; to Eutron for "moderate to severe hypertension"; to Librium "to free the patient from anxiety. . . ." Nervous strain, tension, and anxiety, not to mention depression and despair, are apparently the most ubiquitous minor ills of our society. They are widely taken to characterize "the American way of life." If we were to conclude that such is the case, we would still be left with the equally absorbing problem of why this should be so. But the thesis here is rather to the contrary. Anxiety and despair, as much as confidence and optimism, have characterized our history from the beginning. The anxiety quotient has always been abnormally high in American history. Indeed this higher level of anxiety and larger admixture of despair may well distinguish Americans from all other people in history.

Americans planted themselves in a wilderness, a primeval forest unlike any forest that civilized man had undertaken to subdue for a thousand years. They had to deal with primitives who were often hostile and unpredictable, and they were separated from everything familiar by three thousand miles of ocean. These are, of course, hazards and dangers so well known and so piously reiterated that their full meaning has long since been lost to us. We can recover some sense of these classic and essentially physical hardships through novels like LeGrand Cannon's *Look to the Mountains* or Conrad Richter's *The Trees*. But the psychological pressures are harder to measure. Most prominent among them would be a sense of cosmic loneliness. The settlers at Jamestown died of this loneliness, as we say today, of alienation.

Historians have long been at a loss to explain why hundreds should have died in the first ten or fifteen years of the Virginia settlement. The Korean War gave us, in my opinion, the answer. There a higher percentage of American prisoners died than in any war in our history. They died of what came to be called "give-upitis." They lay down on their cots, pulled a blanket around themselves, and died. Similarly, in Jamestown morale gave way completely. Settlers were unable to perform the simplest tasks. They reacted very much, I suspect, as a group of Americans would today if, as children of an advanced technological society, they were plumped down on some remote and inhospitable island. The first experience of English settlers in America was one of crippling despair.

The New Englanders had another problem. They were armored against despair by their theology and their utopian expectation. But they had, after all, undertaken to establish a novel Christian common-wealth in order to reform the whole of Christendom and that was a rather sobering assignment, one that produced considerable anxiety. John Winthrop's *Modell of Christian Charity*, written on the *Arbella* on the passage to Massachusetts Bay, was the prospectus for a Bible com-monwealth, a company of devout and God-fearing men and women who would raise up a covenanted community to the glory of God. It was, quite literally, an effort to live by the "Law of the Gospel." The Puritans felt that they had entered into a compact with God, that he had given them a special commission:

Thus stands the cause between God, and us. We are entered into a covenant with him for this work, we have taken out a commission, the Lord hath given us leave to draw up our articles. We have professed to enterprise these actions upon these and these ends. . . . If we shall neglect the observation of these ar-ticles which are the ends we have propounded, and dissembling without God, shall fall to embrace this present world and prosecute our carnal intentions, seeking great things for ourselves and our posterity, the Lord will surely break out in wrath against us, be revenged of such a perjured people and make us know the price of the breach of such a covenant . . . for we must consider that we shall be as a City Upon a Hill, the eyes of all people are upon us; so that if we shall deal falsely with our God in this work we have undertaken and so cause him to withdraw his present help from us, we shall be made a story and a byword through the world.

This was the seed of all hope, all aspiration, all tension. In the *Model* we find the archetype of American society, the belief that a better, more godly order of society, a genuinely Christian society like that of the early church could be created. When one has such a commission, it is apt to generate a good deal of anxiety; at the same time, of course, it gives one's whole life a significance and meaning that it could not oth-erwise have.

The Puritans experienced this alternation from hope to despair that is so characteristically American. We find it first in what Perry Miller has called the jeremiads, the fiery, imprecatory sermons of Puritan di-vines to their flocks when they observed a general relaxation of stan-dards among them. Puritans are sometimes thought of as a smug and hypocritical tribe, sure of their own sanctity, censorious of the "strangers," those outside the covenant. To the contrary, they lived, most of them, in an agony of doubt about their state of grace. Were they pre-destined for salvation or for damnation? Had they received an authentic sign or a temptation of the Evil One? They kept elaborate diaries or ledgers recording their sins and errors, their fears and doubts. Here, then, was the primal anxiety.

But, it may be argued, anxiety is the common lot of man. It is in the face of that anxiety that we muster the courage to be and this condition is the essence of our humanity. But men have devised innumerable in-genious ways to relieve themselves of that anxiety or at least to diminish it. Religion, which in its primitive forms is so manifestly an effort to relieve anxieties by explaining the inexplicable and by propitiating the forces of nature; caste, ritual, the symbolic representation of life and death, what Mircea Eliade calls "the myth of the eternal return," all of these have been a profound consolation for the people of many cul-tures.

In Western history the Roman Catholic Church has been, among other things, an extraordinarily rich system of consolation, it might be argued the greatest created by the human imagination. Much of the civil polity of Western man worked to the same end. The majesty of kingship, the style of classes, the marvelous pageantry of office added to the festivals of the church and gave infinite consolation to men on their journey through life. Custom, ritual, symbol, and the sanctifi-cation that time gives—all these things sustained and comforted West-ern man, diminished his anxieties, softened his despair.

In America all these things were lacking. The reformed church de-nied its members the comforts of liturgy and ritual. There was no art, no magic representations of life, no great visions given substance by the artist's imagination, and even, for quite a time, no music; no festivals, no great outpourings of emotion, of dionysiac release from austerity, no great celebrations in which man's triumphs and agonies were symbol-ically represented. Indeed, our common life continues to be impover-ished by the lack of such wholesome occasions.

What was there in the place of all these things? What system of con-solation? What means for relieving the immemorial anxieties of men? For lifting up those who despaired? The answer is, of course, virtually nothing. The family, the community, and the Will, the naked and fearful Will which said we shall inhabit this inhospitable earth, we shall make it flower and bear fruit. We shall make it a plain and simple celebration of the Lord, direct and immediate, shorn of all systems and forms of consolation, naked to the eye of the Lord.

This country was thus conceived and born in anxieties of a particularly excruciating kind. But that was, after all, long ago. The Puritans prospered; the Virginia settler was transformed into the landed squire, the very picture of gentlemanly leisure and pleasant living.

But the anxiety remained and in some ways perhaps it grew worse. It grew worse because the direct involvement of the individual with God began to break down. And the anxiety that followed was undoubtedly more destructive in many ways than the God-produced anxiety. The breakdown was, in itself, of course, a source of great anxiety, a generalized and thus particularly devastating form of anxiety.

These are, in essence, a series of hypotheses. They rest, however, on some substantial facts. From the time the Puritans landed in Massachusetts Bay, drunkenness was one of the most conspicuous and persistent American failings. It bedeviled the saints of Boston and Salem quite as much as it does modern Americans. We understand that unmanageable anxieties lie at the roots of most alcoholism—of drunkenness, madness, and what used to be called nervous breakdown. A much less serious but by no means insignificant index of American anxieties was the nervous stomach. Colonial letters and medical handbooks abound in remedies for nervous colic. Chalk, water, and peppermint was one of the most common, not too different in taste perhaps from the various remedies available today. America has been represented as the greatest success story in history, but in fact its story is full of anguish and desperation.

At the time of the American Revolution another anxiety-producing factor had been added to the American scene: competition. A young man in the period between 1760 and 1800 who wished to be something other than a farmer or a minister had, generally speaking, one option— to be a lawyer. There were, of course, some merchants and some businessmen as well as shopkeepers and tradesmen. But the merchant was the only one of these who could challenge the lawyer in terms of pres-

tige and to be a successful merchant usually required considerable capital as well as vast shrewdness and unremitting industry. Even then it
was a precarious life in an economic sense and did not carry the dignity
and status of the ministry and the law, which were learned *professions*.
It was not until the middle of the nineteenth century, or perhaps the
later years, that the businessman could compete with the professional
in status. (Modern polls show that even today the most desired and en-
vied status is that of the professional man.)

Since medicine had not yet risen to challenge law and since law itself
was in the first glorious flush of its eminence, every ambitious young
American wished to be a lawyer. The consequence was that law was
egregiously overcrowded and the competition was fierce. It took John
Quincy Adams, one of the most brilliant Americans in our history,
years of painful austerity before he finally made the most modest living.
The correspondence between John Quincy Adams and his father is
filled with the son's despair of ever establishing himself and with the father's efforts to keep up the young man's spirits in the face of discour-
agingly little progress. Thomas Boylston Adams, another of John Adams's sons, was never able to establish himself as a lawyer and lived off
parental handouts and minor offices. Charles tried and gave up and
drank himself to death. These were the sons of a president of the United
States, connected by marriage to many of the most prosperous and
influential families in New England. When John Adams traveled
through New England riding circuit with the royal judges before the
Revolution, he noted time and again some Harvard classmate or graduate who had fallen on evil days, who had become an alcoholic or a
hopeless misfit.

In other societies in the nineteenth century, competition was muted
or virtually nonexistent. A man was born to a certain class or caste, to
a certain trade and station in life, and that was where, by and large, all
but the most able stayed.

But the mobility and the classlessness that characterized American
life were productive of the cruelest anxieties. Douglass Adair found the
story of Lewis and Clark an instructive one in this respect. William
Clark and Meriwether Lewis appear as classic American heroes. Lewis
was the son of an aristocratic Virginia family, for two years secretary to

his patron, Jefferson. He was a brilliant young man and a superb leader who with his friend Clark made one of the great explorations in history, a model of courage, resourcefulness, careful observation, and physical hardihood, an odyssey which belongs with that of de Soto or Marco Polo; yet Lewis was subject to fits of profound depression. The moment when the expedition reached the Great Divide and its goal was within its grasp was also Lewis's thirtieth birthday. On Sunday, August 18, 1805, having led his party where white men had never been before, he wrote:

I reflected that I had as yet done but little, very little, indeed, to further the happiness of the human race or to advance the information of the succeeding generation. I viewed with regret the many hours I have spent in indolence, and now sorely feel the want of that information which those hours would have given me had they been judiciously expended, but since they are past and cannot be recalled, I dashed from me the gloomy thought, and resolved in the future, to redouble my exertions and at least endeavour to promote those two primary objects of human existence, by giving them the aid of that portion of talents which nature and fortune have bestowed on me; or in the future, to live for *mankind*, as I have heretofore lived *for myself*.

Jefferson made Lewis governor of the Louisiana Territory in 1807. Two years later, on his way to Washington to prepare the records of the trip for publication, Lewis died in a seedy tavern. Jefferson, who knew him best, believed that he had committed suicide, and this was generally understood until later historians tried to make a case that he had been murdered, apparently because they could not accept the notion that this classic American hero had taken his own life.

Many of the figures about whom we know most in American history had deep streaks of morbidity. Anxiety and self-doubt are certainly part of the process of growing up, at least in modern Western society, but I would be surprised if what might be quite properly called nervous breakdown was as often to be found in figures of comparable importance in other countries. John Adams seems to have had something very much like a breakdown a few years after his marriage. James Madison suffered a similar period of profound depression. Lincoln of course was known for a morbid melancholia. We can find some of the same symptoms in John Quincy Adams. I suspect that if we were to look more systematically at the upper classes of eighteenth- and nineteenth-century America, we would discover a high incidence of breakdown and suicide.

The section of the country most free of corrosive anxieties, one might think, was the South with its leisurely plantation life patterned after the existence of the English country squire. But the white Southerner of course lived with the most acute anxiety about servile insurrection. William Styron's *Confessions of Nat Turner* is an excellent reminder that few slaveholders had untroubled slumbers. The brutal punishments meted out to insubordinated slaves are perhaps the best index to the depths of those anxieties. The greater the fear, the greater the repression. Mary Chestnut noted in her remarkable diary that her cousin, Betsey Witherspoon, had been murdered in her bed:

I broke down; horror and amazement were too much for me. Poor cousin Betsey Witherspoon was murdered! She did not die peacefully in her bed, as we supposed, but was murdered by her own people, her Negroes. . . . Horrible beyond words! . . . Hitherto I have never thought of being afraid of Negroes. I had never injured any of them; why should they want to hurt me? Two-thirds of my religion consists of trying to be good to Negroes, because they are in our power, and it would be so easy to be the other thing. Somehow today I feel that the ground is cut away from under my feet. Why should they treat me any better than they have done cousin Betsey Witherspoon? . . . Mrs. Witherspoon's death has clearly driven us all wild.

The repressed anxieties of Southerners over the loyalty of their slaves had their match in the anxieties of the rest of the country about slavery itself. The abolitionists had the thankless task of dragging these anxieties out into the light of day and forcing their fellow citizens to look squarely at them. It is not surprising that they were not thanked for their efforts.

What about the quality of life in the nineteenth century? Was it of a nature to increase or diminish anxieties? The fact that competition and the attendant struggle for success was almost unbearable can again be measured by the extraordinary number of utopian communities that were founded, most of them communist in principle and designed specifically to do away with competition. Charles Fourier and the phalanxes, Albert Brisbane, Robert Dale Owen, the Rappites, the Perfectionists, they arose by the dozens, almost as ephemeral as the visions in which they were conceived, eloquent testimony to a general malaise in American society. Beneath the strident optimism, the boastings, the frantic expansion, were endless defeats and disappointments, pinched and marginal lives, desperate and perpetually defeated dreams. There were a variety of, on the whole, rather grim expedients to suppress the anxieties—temperance, abolition, peace movements, women's rights, new religions and new sects by the dozen, and the frontier revival meeting.

The great wave of central European immigrants in the late nineteenth century was composed of anxious and uprooted people. But their anxieties weighed very little in the balance as against the anxieties they aroused in the WASPs who talked darkly of the "destroyers" and very seriously proposed denying them the vote and making sterilization mandatory. The sociological and scientific journals of the late nineteenth and early twentieth centuries are full of the most patently racist material imaginable. Ellsworth Huntington wrote:

The choicest flowers are those who make the country happier, more contented, purer, truer, wiser, or better in any other way. Such people are called Builders in this book. True Builders are primarily men and women whose brains are well balanced, well directed and active; people of fine temperament, fine intelligence and fine health. Such Builders have subdued the wilderness, created our institutions, developed our social system, and improved human health. It is essential that the world contain the largest possible percentage of people who bear the biological inheritance of the true Builder, and not of the Destroyer. The only way to accomplish this is to alter the birth rate.

The immigrants' anxieties were classic ones and many of them had to do with what seemed to them a moral coldness and austerity which, quite apart from simple racism, corroded the spirit of those who encountered it. I suppose I need hardly dwell on the peculiarly sharp anxieties that Catholic immigrants, who made up a very considerable number of the later arrivals, aroused. I believe that anxieties about the Catholic vote delayed women's suffrage for almost a generation. Antisuffrage literature is full of frightening pictures of priests herding passive Catholic women to the polls to vote as directed by the Pope.

If we use the rough but fairly reliable measure that repression varies inversely as the anxiety, again I think it safe to say that males in the

nineteenth century were filled with anxieties over the efforts of women
to claim a full place in American life. The masculine response to the
women's rights movement is, for the most part, a thoroughly discred-
itable story of vulgar harassment and ridicule.

In enumerating some of the classic sources of anxiety in American
history, we have not mentioned the underlying one: the transformation of a rural society into an urbanized, industrial society. This was, I
suppose, the great trauma, the basic fracture of the modern psyche.
It made necessary all the other repressions, sexual repression among
them. Otherwise it was a burden too great to be borne. In our own time
we are witnessing, I believe, emergence of the repressed anxieties of the
nineteenth century. We suffer from what used to be called an "efflorescence," from a wild excess of feelings and appetites, and from a simple-
minded enlightenment faith in the "natural man."

The Puritans, as we have seen, had a full complement of anxieties.
It was they, after all, who undertook the novel experiment of living by
Will rather than by custom, tradition, and all the accumulated and intricate forms of consolation that we have devised to lessen the anguish
of existence. But they looked their anxieties squarely in the face, so to
speak. For all the extraordinary things that Americans have accomplished they have paid and continue to pay a heavy but, one hopes,
bearable price. The anxiety, despair, the loneliness, failure, and frus-
tration, indeed, the real terror, which are an inescapable part of that
story must all be faced as the precondition for creating a humane and
universal order.

The above reflections were first delivered as one of a series of three lectures at the Loyola University in Chicago in 1968. If not exactly a shot
in the dark, the thesis that the themes of anxiety and despair had been
far more common in American history than historians realized was
based on rather scanty knowledge of the period of our history after
1800. I have since extended that knowledge and with it my conviction
that anxiety and despair have loomed even larger in our past than I suspected. One could write a very long essay in support of that thesis. I
have, in my labors in the later period of American history, found very

few individuals who were not, at one time or another, subject to crippling anxieties and periods of deep depression. In other words, I believe that there is a vast amount of evidence to support the proposition that being an American has been, like every other human condition, a mixed blessing.

God's Voice
1976 and the
American Revolution

It has become a commonplace to state that Christianity is (or was) a radical religion, that in comparison with the other world religions it contained a principle or a set of dogmas and doctrines that were intended to work a radical change in the world. That it contained other doctrines that worked to quite different ends is also clear enough. But through much of the past two thousand years the Christian doctrines tending to produce change have predominated over those tending to preserve the status quo.

Moreover, Christianity evidenced a striking capacity for renewal and regeneration so that when the institutional church showed signs of rigidity and calcification, reform movements took place that stimulated change in the church itself. The Protestant Reformation was such a movement of reform within the Christian Church. It proved to be the most radical re-forming of the church in its long history.

Arnold Toynbee has written that the American Revolution was made possible by American Protestantism. That, very simply, is the assumption on which this essay is based. The assumption is perhaps best stated as proposition. The Protestant Reformation produced a new kind of consciousness and a new kind of man. The English colonies of America, in turn, produced a new and unique strain of that new consciousness. It thus follows that it is impossible to understand the intellectual and moral forces behind the American Revolution without understanding the role that Protestant Christianity played in shaping the ideals, principles, and institutions of colonial America.

The American Revolution might thus be said to have started, in a sense, when Martin Luther nailed his ninety-five theses to the church door at Wittenberg. It received a substantial part of its theological and philosophical underpinnings from John Calvin's *Institutes of the Christian Religion* and much of its social theory from the Puritan Revolution of 1640–1660 and, perhaps less obviously, from the Glorious Revolution of 1689.

Put another way, the American Revolution is inconceivable in the absence of that context of ideas which have constituted radical Christianity. The leaders of the Revolution in every colony were imbued with the precepts of the Reformed faith. Even though in many specific instances Christian orthodoxy was modified by Enlightenment ideas, there was a kind of irreducible stratum of Christian doctrines that were shared by colonists of all denominational persuasions or none at all.

When Luther made his dramatic gesture of defiance in 1517, he did more than attack specific abuses in the Roman church; he struck at some of its basic dogmas. He insisted, for instance, that a man or woman could find salvation only through faith. And, perhaps most significant in its effect on the settlers of the New World, Luther held that the individual was wholly responsible for his own salvation.

If Luther was the originator of the Reformation, John Calvin was its most formidable theorist. In his *Institutes*, Calvin presented the doctrinal basis of the branch of the Reformation that, as Calvinism, became the foundation of American Puritanism. The *Institutes* was, in effect, the charter for a new kind of consciousness, a new way of looking at the world and one's fellows, as well as a new way of understanding the relationship of the individual to the Divine.

Before the Reformation people had belonged, most typically, to orders; to social groups and classes, to communes and communities—estates—by which they were defined and which set the boundaries of their worlds and established their identities; they were clerks, aristocrats, priests, artisans, members of guilds, of burghs. No one had to live in doubt or uncertainty about his or her place in the world. That place was defined and codified, represented practically and symbolically in a hundred different ways. If such individuals understood the general principles that governed their places in the earthly order of things, they also had reference to an equally specific set of rules regarding their place in the heavenly kingdom. They were incorporated, part of a social body. It followed that Medieval man did not think of himself as "an individual," he thought of himself as a member of one of the clearly established orders of society. These traditional orders did not so much submerge him as define and protect him. Above all, they contained him.

Luther and Calvin, by postulating a single "individual" soul responsible for itself, plucked a new human type out of this traditional "order" and put him down naked, a re-formed individual in a re-formed world.

The doctrine of a "priesthood of believers" with each person responsible directly to God for his or her own spiritual state brought new burdens for the individual psyche but it brought remarkable new opportunities as well. The individuals who formed the new congregations established their own churches, chose their own ministers, and managed their own affairs without reference to an ecclesiastical hierarchy. Thus there appeared modern man, an introspective, aggressive individual who was able to function remarkably well outside these older structures that had defined people's roles and given them whatever power they possessed.

What this transformation meant was an almost incalculable release of new human energy into the stream of history. Put another way, Luther and Calvin invented the individual, and these individuals, at least relatively secure in their relationship to God and confident of their own powers, worked remarkable changes in the world. This new individual proved almost equally adept at founding new sects and denominations as well as new financial enterprises and, indeed, entire new communities. One of the obvious by-products was the notion of a contract entered into by two people or by the members of a community amongst themselves that needed no legal sanctions to make it binding. This concept of the Reformers made possible the formation of contractual or, as the Puritans called them, "covenanted" groups formed by individuals who signed a covenant or agreement to found a community. The most famous of these covenants was the Mayflower Compact. In it the Pilgrims formed a "civil body politic" and promised to obey the laws their own government might pass. In short, the individual Pilgrims invented on the spot a new community, one that would be ruled by laws of its making.

The Reformers maintained that the Roman Catholic Church, by reserving to itself—to its priests and functionaries—all the doctrines and teachings of the Church, had kept people locked up in rituals and ceremonies, which, as Calvin put it, condemned "the miserable multitude" of believers to "the grossest ignorance." "Faith," Calvin went on, "consists not in ignorance, but in knowledge. . . ." The faithful must know at first hand the word of God. The only infallible way of knowing God's word was to read and study it as it appeared in Holy Scripture. Thus it followed that knowledge rather than authority was essential to an enlightened faith. The importance of the Reformers' emphasis on the literacy of all the faithful was recognized by Massachusetts lawyer-patriot John Adams:

They [the Reformers] were convinced from history and their own experience that nothing could preserve their posterity from encroachments of the two systems of tyranny, the Roman Church and the English monarch . . . but knowledge diffused generally through the whole body of the people. Their civil and religious principles, therefore, conspired to prompt them to use every measure and take every precaution in their power to propagate and perpetuate knowledge. For this purpose they laid very early the foundations of colleges . . . and it is remarkable that they have left among their posterity so universal an affection and veneration for those seminaries, and for liberal education, that the meanest of the people contribute cheerfully to the support and maintenance of them every year. . . . So that the education of all ranks of people was made the care and expense of the public in a manner that I believe has been unknown to any other people ancient or modern.

One of the most fundamental changes wrought by the Reformation was to give the family unit an importance that it had never enjoyed before. In the new, re-formed family the father assumed the priestly duties once performed by the church. He usually led family prayers, read the Bible aloud in the vernacular, and even assumed certain teaching responsibilities. The family, as the essential unit and center of Christian life, took on a new dignity and power; it was as though the power of the institutional church had been divided up among the reconstituted families of the Protesting faith.

This change in the family also promoted the freedom of the individual. In doing so it served to release new energies in society, to create new enterprises and new wealth. In traditional European societies, sons characteristically expressed their loyalty to their fathers by following the same trade or calling. But since the son in the new family learned the most crucial truths—those necessary for the salvation of the soul— from his father, he was relieved of the burden of loyalty in other spheres, becoming free to go beyond his father in terms of his own worldly ambition. If his father was a carpenter or farmer, the son might aspire to be a lawyer or a merchant without feeling that he was rejecting his father. On the contrary, the son might best express his gratitude for his father's guidance by going beyond what his father had achieved. The result was a great increase in what we have come to call social mobility.

The impetus to get ahead in the world grew out of the new faith. Calvin placed great emphasis on the work a man did as a way of serving and pleasing God. Work was not a sure road to salvation, for Calvin was a strict predestinarian—that is, he believed salvation was bestowed by God according to His inscrutable plan and could not be earned by either faith or works. But to work conscientiously and well at any task, however menial, was to praise and bear witness to the goodness of the Lord. The consequences are familiar. Protestant countries, and perhaps most characteristically America as the most Protestant of all countries, have been work oriented. Work has been the major American preoccupation or indeed obsession, an avenue to secular salvation, a vindication of the individual and of individualism itself.

Closely related to the ethic of work was Calvin's view of time. Time was seen as an arena in which one worked out so far as possible one's own salvation. All time was impregnated with the Divine Spirit. Everything done in time and with time came under God's scrutiny. None of it was private or neutral or unobserved. Time must, therefore, be used carefully, prudently, profitably, devoutly, every hour and every minute of it accounted for and none wasted. Benjamin Franklin produced dozens of aphorisms exalting this concept: "early to bed and early to rise," "the Devil makes work for idle hands." Indeed, Americans like Franklin often seemed to feel that work (and its hoped-for concomitant, money) was a surer path to salvation than piety.

This typically American attitude toward time had important ramifications and consequences. The notion of time as God's time—time
that had to be filled up with useful activity and regularly accounted for
to God—created a vast new source of human energy. In America it resulted in an "energy pool" that made possible the domesticating of a
wilderness in a remarkably brief time. Perhaps above all, it robbed the
future of its menace. Future time, because it was God's time, was not
threatening, not full of danger and uncertainty, but full of promise, full
of the expectation of the revealing of God's plan for man, and of man's
faithful response. The Federal Constitution was in this sense a monu-
ment to the reformed consciousness. This new sense of time as potentiality was a vital element in the new consciousness that was to make a
revolution and, what was a good deal more difficult, form a new nation.

Austerity, reserve, self-denial were also demanded by Calvin. The
Reformer took thought for the morrow; he laid something by to care for
himself and his less fortunate fellows. He enjoyed the good gifts of God
but with restraint. In Calvin's words, good Christians "should indulge
themselves as little as possible. . . . They should perpetually and reso-
lutely exert themselves to retrench all superfluities and to restrain luxury; and they should diligently beware lest they pervert into impediments things which were given for their assistance." Calvin did not
require excessive austerity; that would have been a denial of the bounty
and generosity of the Maker. But license was a sinful perversion of
means into ends.

Such preoccupations led, quite naturally, to an extreme degree of
self-consciousness and introspection. Those present-day Americans
who are constantly examining the state of their psyches are, in this respect at least, descendants of the Puritans. The faithful Reformer spent
an inordinate amount of time in a painstaking audit of his state of grace
or gracelessness. He frequently kept a diary or journal in which he recorded every step forward and every dismal backsliding, a ledger of
moral debits and credits, often writtten in cipher to preserve its secrets
from prying mortal eyes. Even Cotton Mather, one of the greatest of the
late Puritan leaders, confessed to his diary that he was tempted to "self-
pollution," suicide, and blasphemy, was full of doubts and on occasion
uncertain of the existence of God and of his own salvation.

We might thus say that the Reformer set out on the lonely and difficult task of learning and doing God's will. "Not my will, but Thy will,
O Lord, be done," he prayed. If he did not always understand God's will
or was not able to conform to it, he learned to live, to a remarkable and
perhaps unprecedented degree, by his own will. This self-willed struggle proved to be an unusually demanding, endlessly challenging, and
often exciting enterprise.

The Reformation left its mark on every aspect of the personal and
social life of the faithful. In the family, in education, in business activity, in work, in community, and, ultimately, in politics, the consequences of the Reformation determined American history. The "faithful" were, to be sure, most prominently located in the New England
colonies, but they were by no means confined to that region. The Con-
gregationalists were the classic Puritans in doctrine and church polity,
but their Presbyterian neighbors were just as surely Calvinists. Quakers
might differ in matters of theology, but they were perfect examples of
new consciousness produced by the Reformation, in some matters more
Puritan than the Puritans. The Baptists believed in infant baptism,
which was an anathema to other denominations; the Methodists were
more rigorous about the indulgence of the senses; the Anglicans more
tolerant (or less pious depending on the point of view). The German
Lutherans in Pennsylvania, like their master, eschewed the world as did
the other pietist sects (most of them German in origin), the Mennon-
ites, Dunkards, Moravians. From the austerest Quaker to the most prof-
ligate Anglican was an extended social and theological journey to be
sure. But all along that spectrum of Reformed Christianity one could
find common denominators more important than all the differences.
All partook of the re-formed consciousness.

Today we are perhaps most aware of the negative aspects of that consciousness or character-type that we understand to be our heritage from
the Reformation. It is depicted as sour, austere, repressive, materialis-
tic, competitive, anxious, arrogant, authoritarian, both defensive and
aggressive, inhibited, excessively individualistic. And it may well be
that the creative potentialities in that consciousness have been mined
out, that what we presently experience in such a negative way are the
unattractive residues that remained when the Puritans' zealous faith

and passionate desire to redeem the world for the glory of God had dwindled away.

Remote or repugnant as Puritanism may be to us today, the Reformation in its full power was one of the great emancipations of history. Those who drew together under the new revelation unquestionably felt themselves filled with the grace of God and experienced the joy of creation in its deepest sense. Those who embraced the Reformed faith were, or at least felt themselves to be, truly liberated; they entered into a genuinely new world of the spirit and received in consequence the power to establish a geographically new world. The Reformers were not simply men and women who subscribed to a set of theological propositions, most of which seem thoroughly uncongenial or obscure to us today. They were men and women, individuals in a quite new sense, with a transcendent vision and the passionate determination to transform the world in accordance with that vision.

The political consequences of the social attitudes engendered by the Reformation can be clearly seen in the English Civil War. The resistance of the radical Protestant elements in the British Parliament led to the Long Parliament, the overthrow of the Court party and, eventually, the beheading of the King and the dictatorship of Cromwell. In this strange and bloody episode all the radical political propensities of the Reformed faith welled to the surface. The Presbyterian and Puritan leaders in Parliament were comparatively mild in their doctrines when compared with the Diggers, Levelers, and Fifth Monarchy men. The Diggers asserted: "*England* is not a Free People, till the Poor that have no Land, have a free allowance to dig and labour on the Commons," that is, the public land, and Gerald Winstanley argued that the earth was a "common treasury of livelihood to whole mankind, without respect of persons." "The Community of Mankind" was the first community composed of all those joined in "the unity of spirit of Love, which is called Christ in you, or the Law written in the heart, leading mankind into all truth, and to be of one heart and one mind." The second was the "Community of the Earth, for the quiet livelihood in food and raiment without using force, or restraining one another." These two Communities were "the true Levelling which Christ will work at his more glorious appearance; for Jesus Christ the Saviour of all men, is the greatest, first and truest Leveller that ever was spoke of in the world."

The doctrines of the Levelers, discredited and ignored for more than a hundred years, found expression in the classic phrase of the Declaration of Independence—"all men are created equal." The right of resistance to unlawful authority so clearly enunciated by the Parliamentary leaders and confirmed by the Glorious Revolution of 1689 was the basis on which the Americans opposed the unlimited authority of Parliament over the British colonies.

There was another important respect in which Reformed Christianity manifested itself in the political sphere. It brought with it a revival of the discussion of law—the laws of nature, natural law, celestial law, and municipal or man-made law. This was a heritage that reached back to the ancients and that received its classic Christian formulation in the works of Saint Thomas Aquinas. However, the Reformation aroused a new interest in the nature and sanction of law, especially on the part of theologians of the Anglican Church. It was Richard Hooker, an Anglican divine, who wrote in his *Ecclesiastical Polity* the line dangerous to kings and tyrants: "Laws they are not which public approbation hath not made so." Protestant theologians and theorists incorporated into the political thought of the Reformation the great principles of natural law which were to play such an important role in developing the theoretical foundations of colonial resistance to Parliament and of the federal Constitution itself.

The problem that, as Richard Shaull suggests, remains at the center of all questions about the relation of human beings to the Divine might be termed the problem of original sin versus Christian Utopianism. Original sin involves the notion of an unchanging element in human nature, qualities or characteristics "original" and continuing.

Christian Utopianism, on the other hand, might be said to be grounded in the injunction "love thy neighbor as thyself" and similar "impossible" demands. Christian theology has always been, in essence, a balancing of these claims. In no period of our history as a people have they been more precisely weighed than in the era of the American Revolution. The Founding Fathers, believing for the most part in some form of the notion of original sin, nonetheless dared to believe also in a new and better age for all mankind. Thus the Reverend Samuel Thatcher could declare "Liberty is a pure, original emanation from the great source of life which animates the universe . . ." and assert confidently that the benefits of the American Revolution could not "be compressed within the compass of a few pages. Its effects are not confined to one age or country. The human mind has received a stimulus and attained an expansion which will extend its influence beyond calculation." Americans have, in short, begun the "emancipation of a world."

The federal Constitution was, in effect, an effort to reconcile on the practical political level original sin and Christian Utopianism. In this context the Declaration of Independence appears as the classic political credo of a utopianism whose Christian antecedents are plainly discernible.

The American revolutionary tradition was soon reduced to a reiteration of "freedom, equality, and liberty." Abstracted from revolutionary politics these became, in time, merely pious utterances. Today the challenge of the Bicentennial Era is, as the Founding Fathers most commonly put it, to return to *first* principles. For the Christian the most important of these principles is that God rules the world and that all human orders are merely efforts to emulate the Divine order.

It thus follows that the task of the Christian is always to be *radical* to the existing establishment and *conservative* to secular revolutionaries who, as Reinhold Niebuhr reminded us, are constantly attempting to make their ideals into the ultimate goals of history. For the Christian this is heresy.

The importance of Christianity is as an incommensurable, inexhaustible, (I suspect) irreplaceable, "re-adjuster"—that which *must* survive every social upheaval, every revolution, every war. It is coterminous with history itself or else it is nothing but a system of consolation, another "world religion."

In Richard Shaull's words "the end [in this case the end of the old order of king and Parliament] is the occasion for a new beginning, and men are free to allow the old to die in trust that out of that death, the new will emerge." This is faith in the future as governed by God's will which, even if men cannot discern it, is there; this is the primary, original source of all "utopian" thinking: the future will be better than the past.

The Bicentennial Era, which has so discomforted academic historians, poses equally difficult questions for the Christian community. If the American Revolution is indeed inconceivable without the imperatives of radical Christianity, what does this fact suggest about the Church (or churches) today? How is the complacent and conservative body of Christians to be aroused from its lethargy and made an active agent of The New Age?

Russell Kirk
| 1955 | and the New
Conservatism

In the aftermath of World War II an intellectual movement that termed itself
"the new conservatism" emerged. Led by Peter Viereck, Russell Kirk, and
William Buckley and finding its journalistic voice in the National Review,
it expressed a rather widespread disillusionment with liberal principles and
radical causes. Still reacting to my disenchantment with Marxism (Robert
Frost wrote that he was never radical when young for fear of being conservative when old), I was attracted by the rhetoric of the New Conservatism (it
was soon capitalized). Apparently under the impression that I had become a
believer, the organizer of a discussion on the New Conservatism for a meeting
of American historians invited me to comment on Russell Kirk's "Bible" of
the movement.[1] Under the impression that I was a believer, I consented, but
when I sat down to think in a consistent and serious way about the book I discovered I was a skeptic. My skepticism, expressed in this essay, offended those
trying to establish a conservative orthodoxy, but it freed me from any lingering
disposition to think of myself as one of their company. The essay that follows
this was written many years later when another "new conservatism," commonly called "neo-conservatism," made its appearance, led this time by a
band of former "leftists," most prominent among them Irving Kristol, Na-
than Glazer, and Seymour Lipset. As it suggests, they undertook to appropriate American history and specifically the Bicentennial of the American
Revolution for the conservative cause. This seemed to me patently absurd.

When Russell Kirk's The Conservative Mind was published, its appearance was greeted with delight by champions of conservatism every-

---

[1]Russell Kirk, The Conservative Mind: From Burke to Santayana (Chicago: Regnery,
1953).

where. *Time* and *Fortune* carried lengthy reviews in which Mr. Kirk was eulogized as the gifted enunciator of true conservative doctrine. Liberal journals attacked Mr. Kirk's book sharply, but between the extremes of right and left a number of reviewers expressed qualified approval, often less for Mr. Kirk's ideas than for their somewhat portentous notion that the book marked the emergence of a real American conservatism.

The Conservative Mind is skillfully written with much rhetorical glitter and many witty if ill-tempered thrusts at traditional liberalism. Since its publication, it has enjoyed, for a book of its kind, a remarkable success. It has gone through several printings, sold some 20,000 copies, and is about to appear in two new editions, one in England, and the other as a textbook here. Doubtless it will soon be dispensed as a paperback in every drugstore. Mr. Kirk has, as a result of the book's success, emerged as the messiah of the new conservatism, while an earlier prophet, Peter Viereck, is revealed as a somewhat reluctant John the Baptist.

Many of the ideas that Mr. Kirk has put forth have, at this moment, a most seductive quality. There is general agreement, even among ardent liberals, that we need "a healthy American conservatism." At the same time many young academics have undergone considerable disillusionment with liberalism, and this disillusionment makes them especially susceptible to ideas such as those presented by Mr. Kirk. His elevation to the status of a major exponent of conservatism and the apparent readiness of many people to accept *The Conservative Mind* as a kind of testament of the new conservative faith perhaps make it worthwhile to point out how unsubstantial is the book itself, how spongy and inept much of the thinking that has gone into it, and how inadequate the work finally is as an effective statement of the philosophy and the practical tasks of conservatism in this age.

The first and in some ways the most serious charge I would bring against Mr. Kirk, and indeed against many of his fellow conservative theorists, is his lack of a genuine sense of history. A conservatism without a deep sense of history lacks an essential prop. Ironically, the conservatives have inherited their faulty historical understanding from the very liberals they abhor.

In *The Conservative Mind* Mr. Kirk gives ample evidence of having eaten of the apple of the liberal historical fallacy, which was to assume that there is, at least within a particular culture, a set of ideas that can be identified with the TRUTH and that is equally relevant for all times. The English Whig historians and their American counterparts have generally argued that the meaning of English and American history could be found in the gradual development of certain liberal political and social ideas. Mr. Kirk and his fellows now simply reverse this process and replace the liberal dogmas with conservative ones that are, if anything, more rigid and unrealistic than their liberal counterparts. The folly of the liberal historians has been to maintain that when society conformed to certain liberal postulates it would be the good society. For this liberal illusion, which reduced the fantastic complexity of life to a few comforting maxims, the new conservatives have nothing but scorn, yet when they become programmatic, they do the very same thing that they have charged their enemies with. They offer us a jugful of miscellaneous ideas labeled "conservative thought" and tell us that we must take the mixture for our own good—it is the only thing that will cure us. But we do not swallow ideas like medicine. Ideas exist in tension and must prove themselves in competition with other ideas. They are not counters in an intellectual poker game; they are the responses of living men to the crises of their times. And so they must be judged—by their historic effects, not by reference to some archetypal truth. But the new conservatives do not know this. They are idealists, Hegelians, for whom the only realities are those ideas that they have poured into their conservative jar. The measure of their historical obtuseness is found in their assumption that while the questions are different in different ages, the answers are always substantially the same. As Mr. Kirk puts it, "Real harmony with natural law is attained through adapting society to the model which external law, natural, physical, and spiritual, sets before us." If this were true we could transmute spiritual absolutes into political and social absolutes and stabilize the world, ruling out the danger and inconvenience of change. But since all the experience of history contradicts the idea of a static society, Mr. Kirk is forced back on the image of history as a "roulette wheel." "There is truth," he writes, "in the old Greek idea of cycles." Thus the temptation that confronts the new conservatism is the same that has tempted decadent liberalism—a return to the sterile cycle of classic paganism, à la Spengler and Toynbee.

The historical technique of the new conservatives is similar to that of the old liberals. There are, in this view, good ideas and bad ideas, and there are good men and bad ones (depending largely on the ideas they hold). Since history has an inherent logic and man affects his own destiny, the good ideas must produce good while the bad ideas produce evil. All progress and wisdom are thus attributed to the "good ideas" and their promulgators, and failure, error, and tragedy are simply due to "bad ideas" and, to a lesser extent, to bad men. (*The Conservative Mind* can, indeed, be read as a modern morality play.) But such judgments are at variance with the deeper historical insight that we might reasonably expect of the conservative, which recognizes that good comes out of bad, and bad out of good (assuming that we could agree on those terms) in the ultimately inscrutable course of history; that the road to hell is paved with good intentions and good ideas; and that all ideas, good or bad, are given an opportunity to prove themselves in history. Thus it is no service to abuse Condorcet for having a distressingly naive view of the nature of man. We might better ask what the function of such enlightenment heresies was in history. Did they not result in the extraordinary broadening and deepening of our view of social responsibility? Have they not had at least a partial justification in our present ideals of social justice and universal education?

The new conservatives have recently made some interesting and indeed spectacular reappraisals of individual conservatives as a part of their conservative revisionism, but the limited nature of their technique is revealed when they tackle a broader span of history. Here they skip from one great conservative figure to another, often leaping decades in their dexterous and agile dance, making witty asides about the desperate plight of nations dominated by liberal ideas. At few points do they pause to consider the relation of the ideas they espouse to the political and social history of a particular era, and when they do the results are often distressingly bad. It seems to me that *The Conservative Mind* reveals very well the grosser failings of this conservative revisionism.

Mr. Kirk bases his political and philosophical system on Burke. One may admire the English theorist and still doubt whether Edmund can, any more than Thomas, bear the entire meaning of human experience in his head. But once Mr. Kirk has established Mr. Burke as his archetypal political theorist, he then fashions a bed on which he forces all subsequent political and social theorists to lie.

It is no accident, moreover, that Mr. Kirk begins his story with Burke. By doing so he can ignore a tragic dilemma of English history that one dares to say could not have been resolved in reasonable conservative terms, but had rather to be fought out. "That real Jacobinism never has come to Britain or America," Mr. Kirk writes, "is in some considerable measure the work of Edmund Burke's conservative genius." These are the words of a confirmed idealist. Britain had its own Jacobinism in the Civil War of 1640, which indeed made Mr. Burke possible. He was a child of the Great Rebellion as surely as Saint-Simon and Comte were children of the French Revolution.

Mr. Kirk further assures us that "not a single formidable rebellion has occurred in England since Burke retired from politics—nothing worse than riots and eccentric conspiracies." One cannot but admire the aplomb with which Mr. Kirk waves aside the whole Chartist movement and the radical unrest of nineteenth-century England. In his world there are no burning ricks, no starving unemployed, no Peterloo, no Speenhamland system of rates in aid of wages, just tidy conservative principles preventing an anarchy invited by liberal errors.

Yet Mr. Kirk makes one admission that is perhaps fatal to the infallibility of his hero. "It is one of the few charges that can be preferred successfully against Burke's prescience," he writes, "that he seems to have ignored economic influences spelling death for the eighteenth-century milieu." Might one be excused for asking if there could have been a more serious flaw in Burke's "prescience"?

And how are we to assess the course of English history in the past century? George M. Trevelyan writes, "The task awaiting [nineteenth-century statesmen] under the later monarchs of the House of Hanover was to adapt the system of parliamentary government to the new social facts created by the Industrial Revolution. . . . A failure to make the adjustments [the admission of the middle and then of the working class as partners in control of the political machine] would have led to the breakdown of the system and a war of classes." But this is not Mr. Kirk's view. For him the century is simply a heart-breaking and often, as in the case of the Reform Bill of 1832, a cowardly retreat from the high tide of Burkean politics. He can take this view because he is an idealist. To an idealist the only important things are ideas, and the only important thing about ideas is to keep them pure. As the ideas issued from the brain of Burke, they were pure as water from a mountain stream. Mr. Kirk is horrified to see them contaminated by the muddy stream of history.

He yearns for Burkean figures to lead us, an aristocracy who "through their devotion to the accumulated wisdom of the past, their loyalty to everything old, settled and lofty in society" can be relied on to transcend narrow selfishness and act for the good of all of us who struggle below in darkness. But I wonder if Mr. Kirk can tell us how his conservative aristocrats are to escape the stain of that original sin which he is so ready to impute to the mass of mankind. They must certainly operate under a special dispensation, because the noblest reason is capable of self-delusion and the most high-minded rulers are corruptible.

Mr. Kirk's conservative revisionism does not stop with nineteenth-century England. Speaking of the French Revolution, he writes, "even the Old Regime could have been preserved and reformed without indiscriminate destruction, granted a little patience and good conduct."

When we move to America, Mr. Kirk's technique is the same. John Adams is the American Burke, and all that is good in American political thought is the work of John Adams. When Mr. Kirk declares that "more than anyone else [Adams] kept the American government one of laws and not of men," he so overstates the case for the New England politician that he robs it of all possible meaning.

Faced with the rather embarrassing fact, for his theory, that Adams was not a delegate to the federal Convention, Kirk implies that Adams's turgid book, *A Defence of the Constitutions of Government of the United States of America*, influenced the delegates so strongly that their handiwork can be considered largely an expression of Adams's ideas. But this is not the case. There is no evidence that Adams's book had an important influence on the debates, and a careful reading of Madison's journal will tell quite another story.

John Adams was, by many of Mr. Kirk's standards, a conservative (by some he was not), but his influence on American conservative thought cannot be compared with that of Hamilton (who fails to satisfy Mr. Kirk's requirements for a conservative hero), or with that of James Madison (who was an abler and more realistic political theorist).

If John Adams has a secure place in the conservative hagiography, his son, John Quincy, fares less well. He is cast out of heaven because he is tainted with nationalism (the creeping socialism of the early nineteenth century), abolitionism, and other liberal heresies.

The inheritors of Adams's mantle are John Randolph and John C. Calhoun. These are conservatives with the aristocratic agrarian bent that so appeals to Mr. Kirk—landed gentry, in other words. The fact that they expended their considerable talents in defending the indefensible institution of Negro slavery bothers Mr. Kirk not a whit. For him it is enough "to keep clear . . . of that partisan controversy over slavery and to penetrate instead, beneath the froth of abolitionist harangues and southern fire-eating." In other words, a plague on both houses. Mr. Kirk seems to be accepting a form of liberal revisionism that, as applied to the Civil War, enjoyed considerable popularity in the 1930s. If all parties to the dispute had simply been more reasonable and obedient, if they had left the delicate business in the hands of wise and farsighted leaders (like Calhoun and Webster?) without intruding their own disorderly passions into the affair, everything could have been worked out satisfactorily. The Civil War, it is Mr. Kirk's heartbroken cry, marked the end of the great period of the Republic, the destruction of the landed aristocracy and the rise of crass liberal materialism.

Almost without exception Mr. Kirk and his fellow conservatives affirm their support of Christianity (though not necessarily their belief in Christ). One has the uneasy feeling, however, that Christianity is esteemed by them largely as a bulwark of the status quo. We might almost imagine the voice of Lord Bryce exclaiming, "Good heavens, if the masses don't believe in God, they'll be utterly unstable." Further, we get the impression from Mr. Kirk that by Christianity he has reference to the Anglican Church. Certainly he has nothing good to say about the reform efforts of the Evangelical nonconformists in nineteenth-century England, and one suspects that he is not in favor of this kind of Christianity at all. It is difficult to see how Mr. Kirk, if he is a convinced Christian, can say with consistency that "only enlightened conservatism" can save the modern world. Must he not say rather that radical Christianity is our only hope?

When enlightened conservatism invokes Christian principles in support of its dogmas, it reveals that it has accepted the bourgeoisification of Christianity and thereby once again demonstrated its apparently incurable weakness for confusing spirit with historic form. The conservatives cannot have their conservative faith and then place it within Christianity, because Christianity as faith and teaching far transcends any congeries of social and political ideas, whether they be labeled liberal or conservative. Indeed it would seem that this one painful lesson had been learned beyond the need of relearning by our Western world. We have endured centuries of conflict between groups who confused their political aims with God's purpose. Yet the neo-conservatives seem determined to exhume these old specters, to forget painfully learned lessons, to make one party the party of God while the other becomes the refuge of atheists and traitors.

Many readers will be troubled by evidences throughout *The Conservative Mind* of the author's persistent bias against democracy and against all the works and manifestations of historic liberalism. Mr. Kirk is right when he insists that democracy is not and should not be made into the final human good and further that the natural rights that the eighteenth century so exalted are not absolute but must be maintained by equally important duties. But his dislike for liberalism blinds him to the essential rightness and urgency of many of the changes and practical reforms that liberalism championed. The liberal forces of the past two centuries, granted their false philosophies, their shallowness, and their naturalistic spirit, were historically justified in many of the causes for which they fought. At this moment it is perhaps especially important to recall liberalism's "passion for liberty and justice and hatred for all forms of tyranny, injustice and oppression; its humanitarian idealism; its dynamic faith in the possibilities of human progress, . . . its belief in the value and dignity of the human person and consequent insistence on the equal claims of all men to the rights and freedoms—

political, civil, cultural, and personal—which are essential to the development of a full personality."[2]

It is to a considerable degree as a result of this movement that we are today, in Bonacina's words, "witnessing the mass-awakening to social and political consciousness of all the peoples of the earth." We are at the end of a period in which tremendous masses lived by proxy through an elite who exercised the civilizing function. The "masses" have today a sense of hope and aspiration which, however distorted by liberal utopianism, may be the first step toward full humanity. We should not be surprised that the elevation of the masses has resulted in the debasement of many of the finest values of civilization. In part this is the fault of our educated classes who have created and pandered to degraded tastes. The question that faces Mr. Kirk is whether only a comparatively few can live human lives, or whether, if we try to extend this opportunity, none can. Mr. Kirk seems to take the latter view. In light, he suggests, of the debasement of values that has taken place, we cannot run any further risks with the shreds of culture that remain. We must retrench. We must return to the tried and true older forms of society where sound principles and right reason may still create a paradisiacal land in which a natural aristocracy provides the leadership and the masses toil and spin, happy in the knowledge that they are watched over and guided by their betters. And this involves a rejection of a hundred years or so of history.

The fact is that even if we could accomplish such radical surgery, we dare not risk it. Since we cannot discern the form and needs of the society of the future, we have a responsibility in this transition period, when the middle-class mind does not care much for intellectual values, to preserve intact our full heritage. This is hardly the time to start, in a narrowly partisan spirit, throwing out those aspects of the past that do not fit some particular standard of orthodoxy.

At the end of a prolonged essay on the historic forms of conservatism and their betrayal by a soft and decadent liberalism, Mr. Kirk proceeds to paint a brighter picture of the future than one would have expected from his angry indictment of those forces which, by his own admission,

---

[2]Conrad Bonacina, "The Catholic Church and Modern Democracy," *Cross Currents* 5 (Fall 1951), 7, 13.

have done most to shape our present world. It turns out, however, that things are not so bad, largely because of the resourceful rear-guard action of the conservatives against creeping liberalism and socialism. In fact mere survival has given "libertarian democracy," which Mr. Kirk has so often deplored, an aura of tradition, and in view of that he is willing to waive his doubts about it for the moment and rally to its defense as a repository of tradition and order.

We, of course, owe much to our conservative constitution, "the best-written constitution in the world." With it we have "the widest diffusion of property, the strongest sense of common interest, the most prosperous economy, an elevated moral and intellectual tradition, and a spirit of resolute self-reliance unequalled in modern times." But is this confusing? Since the country has been these many years in the paralyzing grip of wooly-minded, power-mad, bungling, non-Burkean liberals, we are rather at a loss to account for our present fortunate state.

Mr. Kirk's program for contemporary conservatism is also instructive. It consists largely of maintaining what we have, while avoiding the dangers of collectivism. To do this, conservatives must rally the agricultural classes (which have been one of the most radical elements in our society and are now the most completely socialized), "a very large educated class" (which we should be astonished to find had escaped the poison of Deweyism), the churches (whose mission is quite different: that is to say the radical reform of souls, not the support of secular institutions however prosperous and enlightened), and lastly "an increasing part of the laboring classes, which are likely to be attached increasingly to a stable society through the share in things which they have obtained." One cannot resist asking here, "Through whom did they obtain this 'share in things' which Mr. Kirk now appeals to them to maintain?" Not even Mr. Kirk would claim, surely, that it was through the beneficence of enlightened conservatives.

As we read on in his program it becomes quite evident that the conservatism of Mr. Kirk, and his fellows, is a luxury that history affords them at this moment. He may now be right, but would he have chanted his conservative litany in 1933? Would he have denied the efforts of the New Deal to ameliorate the effects of the Great Depression, or would he have stood aside immobilized by the conflict between his conservative principles and the agonizing urgencies of what he calls "the dismal years"? If the achievements of liberalism allow Mr. Kirk, and indeed others of us, to be conservative today, is it not fitting that we should be a little grateful or at least a little humble and cease to exalt ourselves as the formulators of sempiternal truth?

The conservative claims, as distinguished from conservative principles, are another form of the monstrous simplisms of our day, which assure us that if we will abandon all doubt and misgiving and accept this or that exclusive and all-encompassing version of TRUTH, all will be well with us and with our world. The danger in Mr. Kirk's book and in the pronouncements of the new conservatives is that at a time when people are becoming increasingly disillusioned with the inadequacies of the old liberal view of the world, they will turn to a set of ideas that are labeled conservative and hope to find refuge there from the terrible dilemmas of our time. Thus when the real battle is for the maturity of the American spirit, we are tempted by an attractive new orthodoxy that contains much less than the necessary truth and that at worst may simply bestow a spurious intellectual respectability upon political reaction.

We Americans would still like to ignore the fact that "everything good has to be done over again, forever." But we had better remember that there is nothing about conservatives or about conservatism that contains any built-in immunity to decadence. The radical triumphs of one age are the conservative values of another, and these conservative values have subsequently to be revalued by another generation, or, if they have become rigid, overthrown. There is in conservatism, moreover, a kind of complacency that tempts it constantly to resign itself to what seem to be the hard and inevitable facts of human pain and want and suffering, just as liberalism or radicalism demonstrates the contrary vice of trying to assert its will over history and thereby committing the equally grave sin of pride.

Actually, the position of the new conservatives is fashioned of nostalgia and despair. They are, for the most part, men of little faith who dare not imagine a future that is not a pallid imitation of the past. Their system is a kind of calcified shell constructed out of vestiges of the past to protect them from the present and to conceal a vision of the future.

Perhaps at the heart of the failure of the new conservatives is their lack of an adequate metaphysic. The lack of such a metaphysic is particularly serious in conservative political theory because of its inherent tendency to glory the status quo or even the status quo ante. Whatever may be said against liberalism, it has been erected on a pretty thoroughly worked-out metaphysic. Contemporary conservatism lacks this basic metaphysic and in the absence of it must rely on a patchwork of Burkean insights, elements of Christian dogma, and forms of historic conservatism.

There are, indeed, three principal ways of viewing the past. The true liberal is, on the whole, inclined to give little heed to the past, to speak of it often as "the dead hand." The past is something to be subdued, a record of error and superstition, or at best a promise to be fulfilled in the present. The conservative mind, on the other hand, harks back to the past, loves it, glorifies it, claims to understand it (and often does), and has faith in its achievements and traditions. The conservative, however, in his idealization of the past is in danger of mistaking the transient elements for the enduring ones. What we might call the post-conservative imagination grapples most successfully with history because it tries to transfigure the past and integrate it in the future in a free and creative spirit. Knowing that historic forms are merely the husks of the once existent realities, it searches out these realities so that they may be separated from the exhausted forms and saved for the future.

We cannot too emphatically reject the dogmas of the new conservatism. But we are fortunate in having Mr. Kirk's book to instruct us. Peering beneath its surface of dazzling rhetoric, we can see quite clearly many of the more egregious fallacies of the new conservatism. If a conservative credo can be effectively stated for our age, and there is much to suggest a need for it, the job remains to be done.

The Revolt
1976 of the
Radical Realists

One of the early entries in the Bicentennial Sweepstakes was a book published and distributed last year by a conglomerate named American Brands, mother of an interminable brood of "consumer goods" from Jim Beam bourbon (1795), through Lucky Strike cigarettes (1856), Pall Malls, Tareytons, Silva Thins, Half and Half Smoking Tobacco, cigars, staplers, padlocks, office supplies, "crackers and snacks," lotions and soaps, prune juice, and applesauce.

The handsomely designed and illustrated book, offered "in honor of the Bicentennial of the United States," is entitled *The American Revolution: Three Views*. The views, you will not be surprised to learn, are of a notable uniformity. Their common theme is that the Revolution was basically a pretty conservative affair. The implication is that its proudest flowers are huge conglomerates like, of course, American Brands. The president of that company included a little note expressing the hope that readers "may derive fresh insights and a deeper understanding of the origins of our liberty" from its pages.

Not likely. The foreword states that the liberty our forefathers fought for was *economic* liberty. (Presumably liberty to exploit others as systematically as the colonists were being exploited by Great Britain.) "Freedom to produce commodities [like bourbon and tobacco] and sell them in this country and abroad. . . . If our revolution had been as passionate, as romantic, and as heroic as we now tend to color it, 1776 might . . . have ended up in animal savagery instead of leading to a new 'political philosophy,'" the editor tells us.

Applesauce! It is difficult for me to believe that the American Revolution was a mild and reasonable and essentially colorless conflict carried out primarily for the future benefit of American Brands and its sister conglomerates (and multinationals, presumably). But it must be said that this idea is not really in conflict with the prevailing interpretations of most academic historians. The passion, the romance, and the heroics which Americans used to believe characterized the Revolution have been pretty well leached out by scholarly treatments concerned more with "forces" and "historical dynamics" than with the acts of real people.

Leaving passion, romance, and heroics aside for the moment—as well as American Brands' mushy little book—I would like to focus on what seems to me the central issue: Were the members of the Revolutionary generation radicals and revolutionaries in the classic sense of those words?

I believe they very clearly were and that there is a great mass of convincing evidence to prove it.

The American Revolution was one of the most radical events in history. It quite literally turned the world upside down. It altered profoundly and fundamentally the way ordinary people thought about their relationship to traditional governmental structures, to "upper classes," to each other, to the "means of production," to other peoples, to principles of justice.

To the British ruling class and to their counterparts in other nations, the ideals expressed in the Declaration of Independence seemed wild ranting. Ambrose Serle, a British staff officer, wrote: "A more impudent, false and atrocious Proclamation was never fabricated by the Hands of Man." The so-called principles of the Revolution were simply blasphemous, demonstrating "the Villainy and the Madness of these deluded People," who acted with a "savage Fury" that made a mockery of all Christian teachings.

What were, in effect, the radical doctrines of the Founding Fathers? First, of course, they were suspicious of all concentrations of power both in government (as the American Brands' book is at pains to point out) and in business enterprises (which its authors ignore). They believed, almost as an article of faith, in at least relative equality of income and constantly contrasted the United States with Europe, where a relatively few people controlled virtually all the wealth.

Noah Webster, the compiler of the first American dictionary, wrote: "An equality of property, with a necessity of alienation [taking property from those who accumulate excess amounts of it] operating to destroy combinations of powerful families is the very soul of a republic. While this continues, the people will inevitably possess both power and freedom; when this is lost, power departs, liberty expires and a commonwealth will inevitably assume some other form."

Almost without exception, the Founders feared the debilitating effects of luxury or, as we would say, materialism, and John Adams declared it as a kind of historical principle that "human nature in no form of it, could ever bear Prosperity." It had always been a prelude to corruption and decadence. They were suspicious of banks and of the manipulation of money. John Adams and Thomas Jefferson, who differed on a number of issues, were at one on this and debated whether banks or large standing armies in time of peace were more dangerous to the liberties of the people.

Benjamin Franklin observed on several occasions that members of society were entitled to "a decent competence"—enough money to provide an adequate living for themselves and their families. However, when certain individuals accumulated money beyond that level, Franklin argued, society had the right to reclaim the "superfluous property" and use it as deemed best for the common good, since "superfluous property is the creature of society," that is to say, it is amassed by virtue of the social and economic arrangements of the society. It had been common practice in every age, Franklin noted, for the wealthy to "protect their property at the expense of humanity." This marked the beginning of "a tyranny."

Jefferson went further. He was so concerned about the tendency of certain individuals and groups in America to take advantage of their fellows that he wished to redistribute land every generation so that large amounts of it could not be sequestered by individuals, families, or corporations. In the same spirit he wrote: "The earth is given as a common stock to man to labor and live on. If, for the encouragement of industry, we allow it to be appropriated, we must take care that other employment be permitted to those excluded from appropriation. If we do not, the fundamental right to labor the earth returns to the unemployed."

Tom Paine spoke in similar terms when he declared: "Man did not make the earth and though he had a natural right to occupy it, he had no right to locate as his property, in perpetuity, any part of it."

It has been said, rightly I think, that the Founding Fathers, however radical, were realists. In that respect, at least, they differed from most subsequent revolutionaries. As realists they had many misgivings about the future of the republic. While they hoped for the best, they were too well aware of the corruptibility of individuals and institutions not to be uneasy about the future of the republic. Certainly their writings abound with warnings and premonitions. The growth of the influence of powerful families and corporations, which many of them witnessed in the decades following the establishment of the federal government, was a source of deep concern to them.

But it was, above all, the misuse of power that concerned them. There are literally dozens of quotations to be culled from their writings to the effect of Sam Adams's comment that "Power is intoxicating. There have been few men, if any, who when possessed of an unrestrained power have not made very bad use of it."

As important as was the achievement of a new social and political order in America was the promise of new universal human order, hence the motto on the reverse side of the Great Seal of the United States: *Novus Ordo Seclorum*—"*The new order of the ages.*"

A Congregational minister, Samuel Thatcher, giving a Fourth of July sermon in 1796, declared: "All Hail! Approaching Revolutions. Americans have lived ages in a day. Pyramids of lawless power, the work of centuries, have fallen in a moment." Thatcher was convinced the effects of the Revolution could not be confined "to one age or country." Its influence would extend "beyond calculation" and result in "the consequent emancipation of a world."

These are the credentials of the true revolution—not to secure advantages for a particular nation or group within that nation, but to remake the world in the name of justice and equality. That was revolutionary doctrine two hundred years ago and it is just as revolutionary today, I fear.

The Founding Fathers (the better part of them) were radical revolutionaries in the most direct and specific sense of those words. Nowhere that I know of did they *praise individualism, rugged or otherwise* (they clearly believed that the interests of the community should at all times be paramount over the *selfish interests* of the individual), or, for that matter, "free enterprise," or "capitalism," or any of the economic principles and practices that American Brands applauds so enthusiastically. They planned and hoped for a society in which civic virtue, equality, justice, and frugality (rather than luxury) would be the principal common denominators.

Perhaps the last word should be Thomas Jefferson's. The founding principles, he wrote, "should be the creed of our political faith, the text of civic instruction, the touchstone by which we try the services of those we trust; and should we wander from them in moments of error or alarm, let us retrace our steps to regain the road which leads to peace, liberty, and safety."

Wyndham Lewis's
1976 | America
and Cosmic Man

Since the most striking achievement in American history has been the integration of peoples from every corner of the globe into one nation, it is hoped indivisible, and this accomplishment suggests to me at least the eventual reconciliation of mankind, it seemed to me that my discussion of Wyndham Lewis's remarkable little book, America and Cosmic Man, *appropriately precedes my reflections on* "The Lessons of American History."

In 1948 an English publisher brought out a remarkably eccentric little book by a remarkably eccentric man—the English essayist, artist, and critic, Wyndham Lewis. The book's title, *America and Cosmic Man*, suggests its principal thesis: "Either the United States is (1) a rather disorderly collection of people dumped here by other nations which did not want them—a sort of wastepaper basket or trash-can; or (2) a splendid idea of Fate's to provide a human laboratory for the manufacture of Cosmic Man. It is, I feel, quite certainly the second of these alternatives."[1]

At first glance this might seem like the old "melting-pot" theory in somewhat more modern dress. And, clearly, in a sense it is—the melting-pot theory given a new life by, of all people, an Englishman, a citizen of a nation not generally very favorably disposed to melting pots and other amalgamations. But *America and Cosmic Man* is a good deal more, and it has always puzzled me that this odd little volume has never surfaced, as far as I am aware, in the consciousness of American histo-

[1]Wyndham Lewis, *America and Cosmic Man* (London: Nicholson & Watson, 1948).

rians and critics. It has never been reprinted, and I have never heard it mentioned in academic discourse.[2] Is it a neglected classic? Or am I as eccentric as the author and thus possibly his only advocate?

Certainly it is an appropriate subject for consideration in the Bicentennial Era, for Lewis, it turns out, belongs to that substantial tribe of Englishmen who have great admiration for the American Revolution.

America and Cosmic Man is preoccupied with the notion that a new human type has developed in America. In Lewis's view,

> U.S. citizenship is something as unique as it is extraordinary; it differs radically from what in Europe is understood by "nationality." The United States is a fragmentary, most imperfect, and in some respects grotesque advance-copy of a future world-order. . . . It is a Brotherhood rather than a "People." Americans have something *more* than nationality. In its place they have what amounts almost to a religion; a "way of life." It is one of the most important spiritual phenomena in the world today. . . . American citizenship takes with it of course a whole system of ethics and politics; of puritan ethics and revolutionary politics. Both the ethics and the revolutionary principles are a little archaic and also dilute.

But the important point for Lewis is that in America the most diverse cults and sects live together in "relative harmony," and the "obstinate bottlenecks of racial and religious passion" have been broken so that the United States is, for the rest of the world, "an object lesson in how to make the lion lie down with the lamb." The "mystique of America is an act of faith in tomorrow, in something vaguely millennial. Such is the nature of the revolutionary universalism of America."

It is particularly that phrase, "revolutionary universalism" (which so far as I know, Lewis coined), that I find appealing. It is most useful, in my opinion, in recapturing the essence of the American Revolution itself. The Revolution had just this spirit of revolutionary universalism that Lewis seizes upon. The universe came into America (instead of America going out to absorb other species.)

There is much else that is illuminating. For Lewis the American presidents are the "High Priests, the hierarchical summit of this politico-religious order [the U.S. government]—the occupants of a magistracy

[2]It had been reprinted by Kennikat Press, 1969, a fact which had escaped my notice.

comparable to that of the Dalai Lama and nothing else extant." Lewis has intriguing chapters on Franklin and Theodore Roosevelt and on Wilson, and his comments on the nature and function of the U.S. presidency are striking. To Lewis, the American presidents only appeared to have their powers curtailed by the Constitution. "They can do what they will to a very great extent; 'get away with' a great deal. But like so many other things in the United States, it is in a sense as lawbreakers that they function. . . . All the really enjoyable, first-class power of a U.S. President is stolen power: hijacked or bootlegged. And it is done under the usually complacent eyes of that Constitutional policeman, the Senate."

Another factor in the great power of the president "favouring the development of autocracy . . . is the hero-cult which has grown up around the figure of the President. The most mediocre little provincial politico, once he steps into the White House, as the 'ruler of America' (the words of the First Lady) is spoken about with a quiet intonation by everybody; with a quiet but solemn deference for which nothing but some kind of 'divine right' would account."

It is in his chapters on the three presidents—the three political messiahs of the twentieth century—whom he has chosen as his representative figures that Lewis is at once most perceptive and most devastating. "All that he did," he writes of Franklin Roosevelt, "whether wittingly or not—and much he was responsible for—was *good*. He was, however, the archetype of the democratic autocrat—the 'Tsar' or 'Caesar.' Though—typically—not a New Dealer, he was firmly cemented into a Caesarian power by that remarkable organization [the New Deal]—since Jefferson's democratic societies the greatest revolutionary phenomenon in the United States."

According to Lewis, Roosevelt showed how a modern industrial nation could be "ruled." That was by breaking the power of "big-business." Lewis believed that only an American aristocrat like Roosevelt with his innate contempt for the money-grubbing American society could do so. (Subsequent presidents have either been, like Johnson, businessmen themselves at heart or, like Eisenhower, professionals who were overawed by wealth. John F. Kennedy might have broken out of that circle if it had not been for the Vietnam War and his assassination.)

Finally, Lewis reminds us of "how joyously he [Roosevelt] piloted his way, in the seething sea of unutterable nonsense in which all statecraft in America has to navigate, with a bump here and a bump there, as his administration collided with some hoary absurdity. He understood as no other President had the really irreducible nature of those barnacled superstitions and crazy prejudices which clutter the waters athwart which the ship of State is obliged to direct its course. That rag-time thinking which, in one form or another, since the early days of this century has been recognized as what is most essentially American in America."

Wilson and Theodore Roosevelt, two other "elected kings" that Lewis analyzes, come off far less well than the master of Hyde Park. Lewis has a good deal of fun with Roosevelt's bellicosity. "As to his morbid pugnacity," he writes, "that, under analysis, would be shown to be authentic [as contrasted with his assumed boyishness], of glandular origin, probably. War of any kind was very dear to him."

From TR (the "obstreperous vulgarian") to Wilson (the "Presbyterian Priest") is Lewis's course, and Wilson gets rougher treatment at his hands than either of the others. Wilson is the archetype of the arrogant, aggressive, insincere "luster after power" who disguises his own ambitions and fantasies behind a "progressive" rhetoric. Certainly, Lewis is unfair to Wilson, by any reasonable standard; yet it is not, of course, his business (as he reminds us) to be fair. He is interested in describing the American imperial presidency with the vast accumulation of power that enshrouds it and the determination of Americans to treat it as a kingly office and indulge the use of its vast and generally unconstitutional powers.

Lewis's discussion of the American party system—although not as insightful as his treatment of the presidency—seems to me to be as relevant today as it was when he made it almost thirty years ago. "Party," he writes, "became a game, bigger than all the sports-rackets put together. The money involved is past counting. Reminiscent of the Byzantine factions which grew up around the chariot races in the Hippodrome, it is a parasitic sport draining the political energies of the community." Lewis gives much attention to the often-commented-on similarity between the parties—the absence of any profound ideological differences between them. He does point out the manner in which the party system with its largely bogus differences obscures true differences and allows "a monstrous and morbid form of government by the Few" in the guise of government by the many.

In his discussion of the function of party machines, Lewis points out that they turn their clients into "partisans without principles, 'the solidest kind of voters.' " Thus at the heart of an American's political life lies "*fantasy*. The farcical and violent texture of his life provokes only feebly the ethical and critical reactions which people expect."

Lewis's observations on the ubiquitousness of "graft" in the American political system are engaging. He believes that in winking at graft and allowing their cities to be ruled "by a kind of rogues gallery" Americans have developed "a great appetite for nonsense. . . . All the hens of unreason of 'civilized man' seem to have come home to roost in those parts," because it is, after all, in America that "all the irrationality is being worked out of the transplanted European system. In the process, a great plethora of absurdity is induced." America is, in consequence, the supreme land of publicity, which consists largely of making things seem that which they are not. "American publicity," Lewis writes, "is a bizarre fairyland. It should of course be stamped out, and all of its practitioners hanged, for *lèse majesté* (here Majesty being the People). But I confess to having myself developed a taste for such imbecility, as no doubt a psychiatrist succumbs to the lure of the nonsense to which he is obliged from morning to night to listen." The American indeed lives

some more, some less—inside the looking glass. . . . Politics is a Mad Hatter's Tea Party; and if there happens to be so disturbing a figure as the Mad Hatter presiding, in any walk of life, he likes it all the better. . . . He has, in his daily life, no real Red Queens or Jabberwocks, but he has quite a nice assortment of City Bosses, "gorillas," jailbird mayors, "Tsars" of all sizes, from Petrillo downwards; Movie Stars as "Wolves" (with gold-digging Red Riding Hoods), the Zootsuiter "cutting a rug," and the Killer, pistols strapped under his armpits, worshipped by the little children; the Soap Opera with its gurgling organ; Crooners with their sickly bleat, Radio prophets, screaming like birds of prey;

post-mortem exhibitionism in the Funeral Parlors and the sacrificial "hot-squats" when the law offers up a criminal in Chtthonian [sic] expiation.

The huge corporations were, in Lewis's view, the unrecognized villains of the piece. These "economic empires" were not "visibly represented" in the government, "but their pressure-groups are more powerful than a Party; their money hangs like a mill-stone around the neck of a 'reforming' Chief Executive."

Here is his capsule description of the course of twentieth-century American democracy:

Messianic leadership was a natural result of the building up of the American state-religion, after the Civil War, and the high-priestly function of the Chief Executive. But also it is the constitutional corrective for the discontents attendant upon a highly organized capitalist economy. Post-French Revolution America, impelled thereto by Thomas Jefferson and his adherents, followed the abstract, gallic, ideological path. Then the constantly expanding empire, to which Americans became committed, drew them into a sort of jingo imperialism of their own, in the sweep and surge of which the early idealism foundered.

One of the most notable things about the book is that it gives us a fix (in the traditional sense) on the state of mind in the forties, not merely of a particularly acute foreign observer but of a substantial number of American intelligentsia. Lewis, like many of his trans-Atlantic cousins, believed that the fly in the American ointment was "capitalism" and that America, with the Great Depression and World War II behind her, was ready to throw off that particular incubus and move on toward a destiny more in harmony with the visions of Jeffersonian democracy. Then there intervened a period of what might be called capitalistic efflorescence, an era of such dramatic triumphs in the realms of national and international finance capitalism and industrial technology that all doubts were vanquished or suppressed. In retrospect, that remarkable period of post-World War II prosperity seems highly unsubstantial, a kind of house of cards built, at least in part, upon a foundation of energy use. With that intoxicating (and corrupting) economic expansion came the American arrogance of power that brought, as its most disastrous consequence, the Vietnam War. We might say again, with added emphasis, what Wyndham Lewis said in 1948: "Though productive power has been multiplied a hundred fold, man is no better off. Half the population remain underfed and underclothed."

Lewis is also acute in his perceptions of the causes and effects of the American Revolution. "At the founding of the American Republic," he writes, "the leaders in the War of Independence were bewigged replicas of English polite society. No marked difference to be found there! But the farmers and storekeepers who composed Jefferson's powerful political clubs, the 'democratic societies' (which transformed the new nation from a rather Tory into a sentimentally radical community), readers of Tom Paine and the literature of 'rebel' Enlightenment— these people were really something *new*; it was a novel mixture, at all events."

In his chapter on the Founding Fathers, Lewis writes, "The Republic with its 'rigid' constitution—except for this big hiatus in the sixties, given over to fratricide [the Civil War]—has run smoothly along; chopping down trees, killing Indians, and building up larger and larger factories, taller and taller houses. The 'wild land' of the interior gradually became covered with cities—all much the same." Indeed, American history was so uncomplicated that the historian could "concentrate upon the economic and political birth of this titanic state-organism"— more particularly, the federal Constitution and its great explication, *The Federalist Papers*. This has always been a favorite topic for British observers of the American scene, and Lewis is no exception. "For a political mind," he writes, "it [the history of the beginnings of the nation] is one of the most attractive histories of all: it reads like a lesson in politics. . . . We see the State built up from the bottom as if it were a demonstration in political science." By the same token, *The Federalist Papers* was "the master key to American politics and for the study of the problems of free government everywhere," a "heaven-sent model."

In a chapter entitled "The Beautiful Polarity of Hamilton and Jefferson," Lewis paints sharp portraits of those two remarkable adversaries: "Hamilton . . . a handsome little man, as neat and bright as Jefferson was dim and untidy; an effective speaker, whereas Jefferson was as untidy in his speech as in his gait and dress; excellent in debate, while

Jefferson always shunned it (getting someone else to do it for him; keeping in the background, unwilling to be dragged into action)." And again:

Jefferson was a "cranky" thinker. He looked like a Lakes Poet, and mooched untidily about the Palace at Washington in his slippers. . . . He wasted years rewriting the New Testament. Everything attracted him—Philology, Zoology, Archeology, Architecture, Theology, Literature, and, of course, Politics. His treatises on the pronunciation of Greek, or the Anglo-Saxon language, are said to have been as crankily amateurish as his biological theories. . . . He was a lit-' tle the sort of man who is the laughing-stock or scandal of an English countryside—works on his estate in old dungarees, or builds himself a "Folly." Democracy seems to have been one of his cranks.

And with all his concern for the common man, at least in that preferred form of the Virginia yeoman planter, his view of America as an idyllic spot free from the problems and blemishes of Europe "was a short-sighted, even a self-righteous nationalism." However, "had it not been for Jefferson," Lewis adds, "America would have been a far less attractive place. On the other hand, it is a legacy of unreality [that he has left us], like the dream of a golden age. It serves to deepen the nonsense supervening, when tough politics and cut-throat business masquerade beneath the homespun of the simple farmer, candid-eyed, strayed out of that delectable Rousseauist democracy of Jefferson's imagination."

On the matter of "roots" Lewis is again most engaging. He attacks Henry Miller for his obsession with rootedness and offers a counterdoctrine. He himself feels as much at home in Casablanca as Kensington and feels most of all at home in the United States, "not because it is intrinsically a more interesting country, but because no one really belongs there any more than I do. We are all there together in its wholly excellent vacuum." "The sight of a *root*," Lewis writes,

depresses me; and I know in that country that everyone has left his roots over in Poland or Ireland, in Italy, or in Russia, so we are all floating around in a rootless elysium. . . . [I]t feels just grand to be drifting around in a sea of Poles, Lithuanians, Irish, Italians, Negroes, Portuguese, French, and Indians. It is the kind of disembodied feeling that I like. But to be perfectly earnest. No American worth his salt should go looking around for a root. . . . For is that not tantamount to giving up the most conspicuous advantage of being American, which is surely to have turned one's back on race, caste, and all that pertains to the rooted state?

So America must follow the new path of responsible hedonism, of revolutionary universalism, of brotherhood and fraternity or perish and the best of the world with it. "So-called austerity, the stoic injunction, is the path towards universal destruction. It is the old, the fatal competitive path."

Wyndham Lewis, at the end of his book, returns once more to the theme of brotherly love, "a Rotarian or Lionesque brotherly gregariousness . . . often taking somewhat ridiculous forms, but of the highest utilitarian value."

Lewis intends, he reminds us, to provide a "philosophic background for my running panegyric of that 'rootless Elysium' of the American city: irresponsible, dirty, corrupt, a little crazy," but nonetheless the adumbration of a new human order.

The problem of writing a "review" of Wyndham Lewis, beside the fact that, as I have already pointed out, no one has ever read his book and therefore he must be "viewed" rather than "reviewed," is that, as always true of the best of writers, it is impossible to separate his message from his mode of conveying it. Thus he demands to be quoted. Certainly he has a message, a prophecy of a socialist world order of which he believes America to be a dim prefiguring, but the message serves, in my opinion, only to sharpen his perceptions. In fact he raises, in a very direct form, what we might call the question of "thesis history" versus "objective history." Thesis history in the hands of a person of genuine intelligence and insight is almost inevitably better than so-called objective history—that is to say, more illuminating and, on the deepest level, more accurate, because the thesis directly and plainly stated gives life and vitality to the history. Put another way, *America and Cosmic Man* is a kind of September romance sprinkled with the insights achieved through love.

Whether we are worthy of this eccentric Englishman's late-blooming love is beside the point. Looking at America through his eyes, we see it afresh. His understanding of and affection for some of our less appealing qualities is disarming, especially in a time when we are inclined to be excessively critical of our past and our traditions.

There remains the question, raised at the beginning of this article, of why *America and Cosmic Man* was almost totally ignored when it was published in 1948—certainly by academic historians. The answers are probably obvious enough. It fell under no recognizable historical canon. Its author was not a historian, nor was the book orthodox history, or even unorthodox history. In my view, it belongs with such classics as William Carlos Williams's *In the American Grain* and D. H. Lawrence's *Studies in Classic American Literature*.

On Writing
History

So far as there are any "laws" in history, it is a law that all human institutions tend to formalism. That is to say that institutions, often in a
remarkably short time, pay far less attention to the purposes for which
they were founded than to simply maintaining themselves. They indeed not uncommonly become actual impediments to the achievement of the purposes for which they were established. Anyone who has
dealt with a bureaucracy, political or social, has been disheartened or
enraged by the dullness of spirit, obtuseness, and defensiveness that it
evinces. It should not surprise us then that the writing of history, so far
as it is done by individuals called professors in places called universities,
should be characterized by a high degree of formalism. This formalism
in the writing of history (and here I will concentrate on that field of history I know best—American history) manifests itself by "dead works,"
that is to say, primarily books that are dull and uninteresting (although,
one hopes, scholarly) by intention. They are not intended to be read so
much as absorbed by a kind of intellectual osmosis. Their authors hope
that they will become part of the acknowledged scholarship in a particular "field." That is to say that anyone who wants to know everything
there is to know about a particular topic (which is what so-called scholarship has come to amount to) will find it necessary to consult our author's work. That academic historians deliberately write badly might
seem difficult to credit if there were not substantial evidence to support
the contention. As early as 1906, William James was taking note of the
fact. "Of all the *bad writing* the world has seen," he wrote a friend, Theodore Flournoy, "I think that our American writing is getting to be the

worst." The academic world had "unchained a formlessness of expression that beats the bad writing of the Hegelian epoch in Germany." James was speaking specifically about young philosophers at Harvard and elsewhere but the same was all too true in other academic fields. Professor H. Morse Stephens, indignant at Theodore Roosevelt's exhortation, in his Presidential Address before the American Historical Association, to historians to write better, declared defiantly, "It is almost an insult to an historian of the modern school to say that his work can be recognized by its literary style. It is not his business to have a style." A scientist, recording an experiment, presumably did not have a "style." If the plain, unvarnished truth was the goal of the history, a "style," by which was generally meant some kind of fancy writing intended to appeal to the readers' emotions in a modest degree, was not only irrelevant but positively baneful. Computers had not yet been invented but the ideal work of scholarship, by this manner of thinking, was one that appeared to have been compiled by a machine rather than by a human being.

That sounds absurd on the face of it but aspiring young historians who wrote like machines were favored over those who wrote like angels (the latter in fact were disposed of as quickly and quietly as possible). The results were, in the main, predictable. As the number of academic historians grew, their output swelled to vast proportions; tens of thousands of academic historians produced hundreds of thousands of volumes of academic history but virtually none produced history that anyone could read with pleasure. Of all the volumes on American history written by professors over the past eighty years or so, one would be hard pressed to think of any that had been read by more than a very limited academic audience or that had entered into what we might not unreasonably call "the literature of history," that is, books that could still be read with profit by intelligent readers as well as by professional historians working "in the field," whatever that field may have been. There have certainly been important and influential books and able if not brilliant historians scattered about the academic world, but one is hard pressed to name more than a dozen or so who are outstanding and more than a handful of "greats."

Frederick Jackson Turner wrote a marvelous essay in 1892 on the

"Significance of the Frontier in American History" but he never wrote anything else of consequence. Charles McLean Andrews, the Yale professor, wrote the *Colonial Period of American History* in four substantial volumes that certainly do not challenge Professor Stephens's injunction against any semblance of style. The senior Arthur Schlesinger developed the field of "social history" and taught a stupefyingly dull course on the subject for years at Harvard. His son, the younger (not "junior" as he properly insists), has written some excellent and widely read history. C. Vann Woodward, the doyen of Civil War historians, has written a brilliant and enduring biography of Tom Watson and several other books that are both original (scholarly) and readable. The late Richard Hofstadter wrote brilliantly and for a larger-than-academic audience, but one may doubt if any work other than the *American Political Tradition* will survive.

Allan Nevins was a journalist who converted to the academic world and wrote books that people read or at least, in the case of his nine-volume history of the Civil War, put on their book shelves. Indeed, Nevins established a kind of historical "factory," turning out, with numerous assistants, books at a considerable rate, but readable as he may have been he was certainly no master of prose style. It need hardly be said, he was viewed by his academic colleagues as an exotic.

Towering over all the rest was Samuel Eliot Morison, who was very conscious of writing in the tradition of the great nineteenth-century historians, Parkman, Prescott, Motley, and Bancroft. But Morison was almost alone in commanding both the respect of his colleagues and a considerable public following.

One mark of the tendency of all human institutions to formalism is a preoccupation with "method" and "procedure" rather than with outcome or results. Thus the immemorable bureaucratic cries: "That's not the way we do it," or "That's not the way it's done," or "It can't be done that way." The spirit is weighed down and eventually killed by the "method," the terrible burden of things-as-they-have-come-to-be-and-must-continue-to-be. "No style" was of course not merely a negative injunction; it was part of a philosophy of historical scholarship that hardened almost at once into "methodology" that came to have the force of natural law.

Every prospective historian was drilled in the new methodology as though it had been brought down the mountain from Zion with the tablets of the law. The principal elements in the methodology were footnotes (carefully prescribed as to form), bibliographies (as long as possible, which led, inevitably, to bibliography inflation and fakery), and above all index cards. A fledgling historian had it drilled into him, and, infrequently, her, that he or she must first select for "research" an appropriately limited topic (any generalizing tendencies were discouraged, not of course because "capital," as Brooks Adams argued, feared and disliked the generalizing mind but because it had become "natural law" that serious historians were specialists). So the apprentice historian chose a minute and not infrequently unimportant topic and then applied to it, with the patience of Job, the methodology, which, in fact, was simple enough. It consisted in reading everything of any conceivable relevance to the tiny little topic and writing down on index cards all facts or hypotheses possibly bearing on the tiny topic. The index cards in time took on a fetishistic potency of their own. The accumulation of vast numbers of them, neatly arranged by subtopic, in little boxes, gave the researcher the comforting illusion of having mastered the subject. If and when researchers could free themselves from the nagging fear that they had overlooked something, they began to write, rigorously excluding any quality of style that might hint at a person behind all those laboriously assembled notes.

The beginning of the writing, deceptively simple as it sounds, is often an experience of profound trauma. The researcher not infrequently becomes, in Freudian terms, an anal retentive who cannot evacuate the notes and who grows so constipated that even enemas of exhortation administered by solicitous mentors, wives, friends, and philanthropic institutions who may have contributed to sustaining the researcher through years of note-collecting are unavailing. Such cases of extreme constipation usually die, academically speaking, and are sent to junior colleges in remote regions where their still carefully preserved notes prominently displayed encourage the legend that they are great scholars who, given time, will produce classic works on something.

While it was never formally codified, the general assumption in the world of academic scholarship was that in any sound work the time spent in note-taking should be five times the writing; that is to say, it should take five to ten years per book; anything produced more rapidly was suspected of being superficial, something just tossed off the top of one's head. Publishers were pleased to be able to say on dust jackets things like: "This definitive study of the Wisconsin dairy industry in the critical period 1880–1890 is the result of ten years of exhaustive research." It would be too severe to call this a conscious conspiracy in restraint of trade or, more accurately, in restraint of production, but that was certainly its effect.

All of this brings us back to our initial point. The institution of academic scholarship is not, in actual fact, much interested in history *or* scholarship in the classic sense of that word. It is interested in methodology. It is interested in maintaining its formal procedures intact, of reaffirming the "natural laws" of historical writing, created in the early years of this century, as though they were the eternal verities. "Past history," John Jay Chapman wrote in 1910, "is studied assiduously and minutely, but it is studied didactically, for the sake of a thesis. The writers strive to docket the past, hold it down, and teach something over its dead body." Henry Adams warned his brother, Brooks, that the academic historians would be severely critical of his generalizing study, *The Law of Civilization and Decay*. Professional historians, "like the church and the bankers," constituted "a vested interest." They would fall on anyone who threatened their "stock in trade quite as virulently as do the bankers on the silver men."

All of this is, of course, special pleading. I have chosen to defy the canons of academic history in order to write the kind of large-scale generalizing history that professors deplore. Such history they believe to be merely "popular" as opposed to "scholarly" (a distinction that would have been lost on Herodotus or Gibbon), written to make money and pander to mass appetites. I cannot understand what it is that academic historians, that is to say, professors of history, individually and collectively, think they are professing. What is their "natural law"? What are they doing and why? They think the question merely facetious; I think they are unwilling to examine their own assumptions for the simple reason that their assumptions, once unveiled, would not support their activities.

I write history in a manner entirely inconsistent with the approved "methodology" of my profession and the question that remains is, of course, "Is the result history or merely a personal and eccentric invention of my own; *or* a reversion to an outmoded and discredited tradition?" At the risk of increasing my colleagues' ire, let me say, quite shamelessly, how I do write, or try to write, history.

There are for me two principal aspects of writing history: the subject matter itself and the philosophical (or theological) assumptions behind the subject matter. My initial interest in history was what might be called philosophical. The man who first roused that interest was the German refugee, Eugen Rosenstock-Huessy. He was what is sometimes called a metahistorian, a man who, like Spengler and Toynbee, was preoccupied with the larger meanings of human experience. The subtitle of his most important book translated into English—*Out of Revolution*—was "The Autobiography of Western Man." Rosenstock-Huessy considered the writing of history an essential human activity—like art. "History," he said, "*must be told.*" It constitutes our collective memory. It is the backward axis of what he called "the Cross of Reality." The healthy life is lived alternately, he argued, in the axis of the Cross of Reality. The forward axis faces the future; one arm of the cross represents the inner life, the other the outer or social life. The rear axis deals with the past. We dare not ignore any of the four axes. Moreover, we can only move forward confidently into the future to the degree that we incorporate the past. We thus seek to recover our tribal past as well as our historic past. The historian has the noble task of being custodian of the memories of the race. He remembers for us all what must be remembered.

Rosenstock-Huessy described three forms of history—grateful history, which honors the notable achievements of our ancestors; reconciling history, which binds up old wounds allowing nations and classes, exploiters and exploited, to become reconciled to each other and to feel that justice has been done them; and finally fruitful history, which points the way to a decent and humane future for mankind. So my interest in history was never primarily scholarly or academic. I was never drawn to history as a collection of facts, "interesting" stories, anecdotes, and so on. Nor was I attracted to it as a specialized study. I never responded to conventional historical scholarship with its pretensions to impartiality or objectivity. I believed the universe was ruled by a moral order and that it was one of the tasks of the historian to demonstrate the nature of that order in the affairs of man. Thus I always felt like something of an undercover agent, an imposter. I always wished to write history that people other than my colleagues would read, history that defied academic conventions. I wished to write in as intensely personal a style as possible so that my readers, if I could find any, would have some sense of the kind of person I was and of the context of ideas and assumptions out of which I wrote. I was not interested, for example, in "narrative history" per se. But I did, increasingly, come to believe that a historian's first responsibility, or *my* first responsibility, was to tell *what happened* as fully and accurately as possible, as fairly and compassionately. Moreover, I believed that the teaching of history was not an activity more or less independent of scholarship but an integral part of the study of and reflection upon history.

I was not interested in history as literature or as art. Or as entertainment. I believed it could and should be all of those things as a consequence of being done properly. To me history was a form of revelation or salvation, medicine for the soul. We cannot exist as a people without respect for the past and gratitude for what our ancestors have bequeathed us. The reconciling element is also very important to me. Generations must be reconciled to each other as well as classes and races.

John Jay Chapman, the critic and essayist, wrote early in this century that the emotions of the youth in every vigorous society should be fed upon the great works of the past—"songs, aspirations, stories, prayers, reverence for humanity, knowledge of God;—or else some dreadful barrenness will set in and paralyze the intellect of a race. . . . To cut loose, to cast away, to destroy, seems to be our impulse. We do not want the past."

It seems to me that we do yearn for an "accessible past." The problem for the historian is, of course, how to make it accessible. While it is certainly a risky enterprise, it is, at the same time, disarmingly simple. When my older son was eight or so he came home from school with a friend who looked at my comparatively modest library and said something like, "Gosh, look at all those books! What are they *for?*" And my son, very knowledgeable, said, "My dad writes books and he copies them out of those." Excellent. The thought has been a comfort to me over the years. Gradually I shed the inhibitions my graduate study had instilled in me about the proper historical methodology described at the beginning of these comments. I had one sure defense against the canons of my profession: I was irredeemably lazy. I grew faint at the thought of such labors. My ambition was to read the absolute minimum number of books necessary to make a reasonably intelligent statement about the subject under consideration and write it down as quickly and simply as possible. *With no note cards at all.* And finally with no footnotes and bibliographies. The essential information that they contained should, in my opinion, be in the text itself rather than limping along at the bottom of the page or the back of the book.

Finally, I was convinced from the first that the interesting and important part of history was *what the people in it had said or written.* I believed that what the actors, major and minor, in history had said was far more important than *what historians said about them.* I suppose that if I have one basic article of faith about the process of writing history it is this: *Listen to the voices of the past,* their precise tones and accents, and try to enter sympathetically into their hopes and visions.

So my methodology is simplicity itself. I sit down and read what people said. I copy it down. When I have a pile large enough to make a book I glue it all together to give it some rough coherence, write some sentences to connect the various quotations and presto! easy as rolling off a log, a lazy man's history. I let my progenitors write it for me. I don't know what's going to be in it when I start. No chapter outlines, no topical headings—just an open and reasonably empty mind. *They* (not some professor of history) tell me what should be in the book. They dictate it; I write it down. It is a process full of marvelous surprises and revelations, intoxicating, obsessive. It wakes me up at night; it fills my dreams. By this process I have come to know and love any number of great spirits. William James dedicated his life to "loving affections," pointing out that these may include the dead as well as the living, and this has been preeminently my experience. It has also come to be my dearest ambition for the work I am presently engaged in—that readers will feel that they have acquired a host of new friends, a noble company of kindred spirits, and will have in consequence the sense of living in a larger and more generous world than before.

From Masses
1974 to Peoplehood

Every emancipation is a restoration of the human world and of
human relationships to man himself.

Karl Marx

The excluded or repressed are always right in their rebellion, for
they stand for our future wholeness.

Paul Goodman

We only become what we are by the radical and deep-seated refusal of that which others have made of us.

Jean-Paul Sartre

One of the most striking of all historical phenomena is that by which
those groups in a society who have been in a subordinate, dependent
position, the clients, or more properly, the wards, of the dominant social group assert their humanity. These wards are in a real sense passive;
they have no power and no voice. They belong to "the masses." They
are an undifferentiated mass; their guardians define them, decide and
prescribe their functions and activity. In a certain sense they exist most
substantially in the consciousness of the dominant group. Their task is
to reclaim themselves from their patrons and in so doing to realize
themselves as authentic beings, to claim their full humanity, to acquire
peoplehood.

Who belongs to "the masses," and what is this process by which
masses become people? One fundamental characteristic of a dependent, subordinate group, or a mass, is that it is described by the dominant group. Men described women in the late eighteenth and in the

nineteenth century: women were delicate, frail creatures, constitutionally unfit for the strains and rigors of a man's world. They were deficient in reasoning powers and thus limited to certain duties and functions. They were a superior order, but a superior order of a strange kind whose function was to attend dutifully to the wants and needs of men. And the women were then as men described them. They behaved as men said they must behave. They fainted; they were constantly ailing; they accepted without protest the outrageous and tyrannical impositions of men. It was their nature. They could do nothing else.

The case of black people in the United States was similar. The white man described the black man as lazy, shiftless, happy-go-lucky, irresponsible, deceitful, musical, and so on, and the black man often behaved just that way. The white man, without realizing that he had, in fact, created this caricature, pointed to it as a confirmation of his description of the black man's nature.

The dominant class describes and defines the subordinate one, the mass. The crucial question is how does the subordinate group, the mass men and women, get out of the box in which they have been placed? How do they escape the definition of themselves by the dominant group?

It was during the nineteenth century that women emerged from their historical situation of dependence and subordination in the context of the antislavery crusade. Outraged by the institution of slavery, they joined in the antislavery agitation early in the nineteenth century and the bolder ones among them, like Lucretia Mott and the Grimké sisters, became leaders in the abolitionist movement. Women seized on the fact that slavery was a moral issue; the slaves must be freed, and they must be freed at once. They grasped the nettle of slavery far more boldly than their male counterparts. Angelina Grimké's wedding is an example of the determination of those women who were leaders in the abolitionist movement to live by what they professed. A black minister as well as a white minister officiated at her wedding to Theodore Weld before a mixed congregation of blacks and whites—a shockingly bold proceeding for that day.

Angelina's sister Sarah wrote, "It is the duty of abolitionists to identify themselves with these oppressed Americans by sitting with them in places of worship, by appearing with them in our streets, by giving them our countenance in steamboats and stages, by visiting with them in their homes, and encouraging them to visit us, by receiving them as we do our white fellow citizens." This was not theoretical equality but the effort to live their beliefs in everyday life.[1]

Lucretia Mott, the marvelous Quaker woman who was perhaps the first great leader of the abolitionist movement, wrote that her sympathy "was early enlisted for the poor slaves, by the classbooks read in our schools, and pictures of the slave ship. . . . The unequal conditions of women in society also early impressed my mind." The oppression of the working classes by monopolies, the low wage rates, the inequities of a society in which the rich grew richer and the poor poorer, all these issues concerned her deeply. But slavery was her first concern: "The millions of downtrodden slaves in our land being the greatest sufferers, the most oppressed class, I felt bound to plead their cause, in season and out of season, to endeavor to put my soul in their soul's stead, and to aid all in my power, in every effort for their immediate emancipation."[2]

Another American woman in the 1850s wrote thus:

If ever Africa shall show an elevated and cultivated race—and come it must, some time, her turn to figure in the great drama of human improvement—life will awake there with the gorgeousness and splendor of which our cold western tribes faintly have conceived. In that far-off mystic land of gold, and gems, and spices, and waving palms and wondrous flowers, and miraculous fertility, will awake new forms of art, new styles of splendor, and the negro race, no longer despised and trodden down, will, perhaps, show forth some of the latest and most magnificent revelations of human life. Certainly they will, in their gentleness, their lonely docility of heart, their aptitude to repose on a superior mind and rest on a higher power, their child-like simplicity of affection, and facility of forgiveness. In all these they will exhibit the highest form of the peculiarly *Christian life*, and, perhaps, as God chasteneth whom he loveth, he has chosen poor Africa in the furnace of affliction, to make her the highest and noblest in that kingdom which he will set up, when every other kingdom has been tried and failed; for the first shall be last, and the last first."[3]

[1]Gerda Lerner, *The Grimké Sisters* (Boston: Houghton Mifflin, 1968), 251.
[2]*Eminent Women of the Age* (Hartford: Arno Press, 1868), 373–376.
[3]Harriet Beecher Stowe, *Uncle Tom's Cabin* (New York: Heritage Press, 1938), 119.

Those words are from *Uncle Tom's Cabin*, Harriet Beecher Stowe's extraordinary novel, and they are Harriet Stowe speaking to the reader in the most remarkable literary work produced in the nineteenth century in America. *Uncle Tom's Cabin* could only have been written by a woman. It was of great significance in the emergence of women as a mid-nineteenth-century phenomenon of world historical importance. Beneath the conventional surface of this nineteenth-century romantic novel is a tragic and terrifying story quite equal in intensity of vision to *Moby Dick* or to *Pierre*.

Much of the rapid growth of antislavery societies (there were over a thousand by 1837 with a combined membership of over 100,000, of which women made up a very considerable proportion) was due to the efforts of women. They were the great collectors of signatures on antislavery, abolitionist petitions to Congress. In April of 1838, the abolitionists' petitions received by Congress were reported to have filled a room twenty by twenty by fourteen feet, an estimated half-million signatures, most of them solicited by women.

The antislavery, and more specifically the abolitionist, movement was the means of entry into American social and political life for a vast number of women who organized, attended, and chaired meetings, prepared agenda, made motions, debated issues, circulated petitions, and did all of this in the face of passive, if not active, hostility and resistance from men. To the liberal and indeed to the radical male reformers who were leaders in the antislavery movement, it seemed inappropriate for men and women to work together in the same group or organization. There was from the first a female antislavery society to which women were confined. They were sharply segregated and not allowed to speak or to participate directly in the meetings of the male abolitionists. The women's rights movement was born in 1840 when American women delegates to the World Antislavery Convention in London were refused seating because of their sex. The American men were indignant, and William Lloyd Garrison refused to present his credentials. Finally the women were allowed to sit in the balcony with a curtain drawn so that the men would not be distracted or contaminated by their presence.

The outrage of the American women delegates led to the Woman's

Rights Convention at Seneca Falls, New York, in 1848. The Convention's declaration of independence, modeled on the original Declaration, was drafted by Elizabeth Cady Stanton, who declared: "We hold these truths to be self-evident; that all men and women are created equal. . . . The history of mankind is a history of repeated injuries and usurpation on the part of man toward woman, having in direct object the establishment of tyranny over her. . . . He has endeavored in every way that he could, to destroy woman's confidence in her own powers, to lessen her self-respect and to make her willing to live a dependent and abject life."

Mrs. Stanton almost split the women's rights movement at its inception by insisting on presenting a resolution, against the opposition of a good many of the delegates to the Convention, declaring that women have "a sacred right to the elective franchise." Her father, Judge Cady, when he heard of this scandalous resolution, thought that his daughter had lost her mind. He took a special trip to Seneca Falls to talk to her and assure himself that she had, indeed, stated so wild and improbable a notion. When she admitted that she had, he said, "My child, I wish you had waited until I was under the sod before you had done this foolish thing!"[4]

The reaction of men to the women's rights movement can best be described as hysterical. The newspapers of the day were filled with editorials attacking "these unsexed women who make a scoff of religion, who repudiate the Bible and blaspheme God; who would step out from the true sphere of the mother, the wife, and the daughter, and taking upon themselves the duties and business of men, stalk into the public gaze, and by engaging in the politics, the rough controversies, and the trafficking of the world upheave all existing institutions and overturn all the social relations of life." The *New York Herald* in January 1863, spoke of "these women who would not be guilty of such vulgarity as to live with their husbands. Infidelity and socialism have distorted their heads."

Abby Kelly requested permission to speak at a meeting of the Connecticut Antislavery Society in 1840. When the membership granted

[4]*Eminent Women of the Age*, 347–348.

her permission, the chairman of the meeting resigned his post declaring, "I will not sit in a chair where women bear rule. I vacate this chair. No woman shall speak or vote where I am moderator. I will not countenance such an outrage on decency. I will not consent to have women lord it over men in public assemblies. It is enough for women to rule at home."[5]

The most remarkable aspect of this period, when women emerged from what was very clearly a situation of dependence and subordination, was that they emerged as speakers. In the period from the 1840s to the 1870s, women were among the most popular and effective speakers in the United States. Crowds of people turned out to hear them. They addressed committees of Congress, they spoke at every public gathering, in state legislatures, and in lecture halls. At the end of a tour during which she spoke at eighty meetings in sixty-eight towns and cities, Angelina Grimké appeared before the Massachusetts State Legislature and spoke on abolition: "I stand before you as a moral being endowed with precious and inalienable rights, which are correlative with sound duties and high responsibilities; and as a moral being I feel that I owe it to the suffering slave, and to the deluded master, to my country and the world, to do all that I can to overturn a system of complicated crimes, built up upon the broken hearts and prostrate bodies of my countrymen in chains, and cemented by the blood, sweat and tears of my sisters in bonds."[6]

The women who spoke in public in the beginning of the 1830s and 1840s discovered the power of the word, and they gained an irresistible eloquence as the consequence of this discovery. They became visible where they had been invisible; they became audible where they had not had a voice; they suddenly appeared as vivid and compelling figures. It is impossible for the modern imagination to conceive of the effect that it had on men when women, who had been declared to be frail, delicate, mute, found an expressive and powerful public voice.

The word, spoken with passion, is irresistible. We *must* listen. Women spoke about abolition, they spoke about their rights as human be-

[5]Quoted by Lillian O'Connor, *Pioneer Women Orators* (New York: Columbia University Press, 1954), 36.
[6]Quoted by Gerda Lerner, *The Grimké Sisters*, 374.

ings, they spoke about the cause of temperance; and they spoke with passion, mesmerically. People listened and were thrilled and moved, and the whole notion of what women were, their place, their character, was transformed in this primary and classic public act of their standing up and speaking. As they spoke, they made constant analogies to the state of women and of slaves. We find this in all the rhetoric of the women's rights movement. In much of it there is evident hatred of men. Indeed, the women's rights movement was torn by the question of whether liberal men who believed in the women's rights cause should be allowed in women's rights organizations.

From the 1860s to the 1920s, American women, emulated by their sisters all over the world, constantly enlarged the range of activities, of careers and opportunities open to them. In higher education, in the professions of law and medicine, as teachers and missionaries, in politics and social reform, they carried forward determined and successful campaigns to establish their rightful place in American life. The emancipation of women from their ancient bondage was the most dramatic event of the nineteenth century, an episode of world historical significance, though it is perhaps not surprising that men did not find it so.

The remarkable capacity of women for organizational activity and their passion for social justice enabled them to affect every area of American society. By the end of the nineteenth century hundreds of thousands of women were organized in battalions and armies of reform primarily through two agencies—the Woman's Christian Temperance Union, presided over by Frances Willard, and the women's club movement, which in the aggregate enlisted tens of thousands of women in hundreds of towns and cities. The WCTU was a miracle of organization with forty departments and "ten thousand local unions." Its reform activities extended far beyond temperance to include the institution of proper sanitary conditions in cities, child-labor laws, the eradication of prostitution, improved working conditions for women, and a hundred other good causes. Not satisfied with evangelizing at home, the WCTU formed an international union made up of women of all nations "interested in temperance or social purity [prostitution] or *any other form of Christian, philanthropic, or reformatory work* without respect to nationality, class, or creed" (italics mine). Speaking of the activities of the WCTU in the South, Anne Scott has written, "No group did more to subvert the traditional role of women, or to implant in its Southern members a sort of unself-conscious radicalism. . . ."[7]

The International Council of Women, held in Washington, D.C., in 1888, brought together representatives from twenty-seven countries and a hundred and twenty-six organized groups, fifty-six in the United States. Elizabeth Cady Stanton reminded the delegates that "half a century ago the Women of America were bond slaves. . . . Their rights of person and property were under the absolute control of fathers and husbands. They were shut out of the schools and colleges, the trades and professions, and all offices under government . . . and denied everywhere the necessary opportunities for their best development. Worse still, women had no proper appreciation of themselves as factors in civilization. . . . Like the foolish virgins in the parable, women everywhere in serving others forgot to keep their own lamps trimmed and burning, and when the great feasts of life were spread, to them the doors were shut."[8]

It seemed to Mrs. Stanton with her legions of devoted ladies about her that the future *clearly* belonged to women. "A just government, a humane religion, a pure social life await her coming. Then, and not until then, will the golden age of peace and prosperity be ours."[9]

The rhetoric of the Women's Liberation Movement contains little hint of the triumph of the nineteenth-century American woman in breaking the bonds that bound her, freeing herself from the subordinate and dependent status that had characterized her position throughout much of history. Doubtless many important campaigns remain to be fought by the legionnaires of liberation, but it seems difficult to believe that the war itself was not won almost three-quarters of a century ago. The task of the Women's Liberation Movement is less that of emancipating the American woman than of reawakening her to a keener sense of her own capacities and potentialities and stirring the conscience of a society that still practices more subtle forms of sex discrimination.

[7]Anne Firor Scott, "The 'New Woman' in the New South," *South Atlantic Quarterly* 56 (Autumn 1962), 477.
[8]*Report of the International Council of Women* (Washington, D.C., 1888), 32.
[9]*Report of the International Council of Women*, 35.

The black power movement began among the Negroes of the South in 1955 in the simple action of a black woman. Its first form was action: the boycott, the sit-ins, the nonviolent demonstrations, and its parallel line was speech: the inspired speech of Martin Luther King, Jr.; the speech of Malcolm X, exciting, disturbing, frightening; the speech of Stokely Carmichael, who first spoke the phrase "Black Power." Though it filled whites and many blacks with alarm when first enunciated, the phrase, itself, proved to be irresistible and offers again remarkable evidence of the power of passionate speech. Like the dominant men before them listening to women, the dominant whites felt guilty, alarmed, incredulous, yet found that they could not help but listen to this passionate, revolutionary speech. There has been no such phenomenon in American life since the orators of the women's rights movement began to speak out in the 1840s.

If one accepts the thesis that the Civil Rights-Black Power Movement was above all else a movement generated by black people at that strange moment in history when they were no longer willing to be a dependent, subordinate, degraded group, certain rather far-reaching implications follow. First of all, it would seem to be the case that Northern abolitionists had misjudged the thinking of the slaves a century earlier in supposing that, with some education, they would wish to enter into the national society. The consciousness of black people had been so warped by slavery, had been so profoundly alienated from the prevailing white culture of nineteenth-century America, that black people could not possibly have entered into American life on a basis of equality. They could only enter on the terms of the dominant society, and they were psychologically, by mentality and by temperament, entirely unequipped to enter that society. Seen in this light the story of reconstruction may become more understandable.

Liberal white Northerners, and Southerners as well in many instances, looked, once the Civil War was over, for the rapid integration of blacks into the dominant white society. Thousands of Northerners came to the South to start schools and colleges in order to prepare the emancipated slave for his new role as a free American citizen. There were nine major associations concerned with the education of the freed slave—the American Freedman's Union Commission, the American

Union Commission, the American Missionary Association, the Freedman's Aid Society of the Methodist Episcopal Church, the Friends' Association of Philadelphia for the Relief of Colored Freedmen, the National Freedman's Relief Association of New York, the New England
Freedman's Aid Society, the Pennsylvania Freedman's Relief Association, the Western Freedman's Aid Commission. Among them they dispatched thousands of intelligent and dedicated teachers who established themselves in every area of the South in what was probably the
most extensive organized effort in history directed at the "immediate
education" of a particular underprivileged group.

The freed slaves, like their benefactors, believed that education
would be the magic elixir by means of which they would be transformed
into middle-class Americans. As the editor of the *Freedman's Record*
wrote, "The guard around the tree of knowledge has given them almost
an exaggerated idea of all its wonderful power; and the spelling book
and primer seem to them Aladdin's lamp which will command all the
riches and glory of the world."[10] A contemporary journalist wrote in
similar terms of the Negro conviction that education could "protect its
possessor from the curse of Adam, and insure a life of dignified ease and
gentility."[11]

The enthusiasm of the freed blacks for education waned almost as
rapidly as it had waxed. By 1870, the freedmen of Georgia were reported to show little interest in schools. In a southern city where teachers from Boston had found a warm welcome in 1866, five teachers who
arrived in 1868 were rejected by the black people of the city. The white
teacher in the town of Hamilton complained that the freedmen of that
community had become "so careless about educating their children"
that the school ought to be abandoned.[12]

The encounter between the reforming whites and the freed slaves
was surely one of the most curious in history. The strange, intricate,
secret life of the blacks encountered the generally rather prim and austere psyche of these latter-day Puritans. The white teachers worked un-

[10]"What Ought We to Expect?," *Freedman's Record* I, 8 (August 1865), 122.
[11]Albert Salisbury, *Journal of the Proceedings and Addresses of the Annual Meeting* (Madison, Wisconsin, 1884), 99.
[12]Quoted in Henry Lee Swint, *The Northern Teacher in the South* (Vanderbilt University
Press, 1941), 73.

der the most primitive and disheartening conditions; often they experienced the direct opposition of black ministers who were busy establishing their influence over their flocks and resented the Northern intruders. It seems clear that the enterprise was doomed to failure from the first. More money, more teachers, more devoted efforts—none of these could have affected the outcome. The two kinds of consciousness—that of blacks and that of whites—were basically irreconcilable. The black masses were too fragmented, too demoralized, too lacking in any sense of themselves as genuinely human to be capable of that ready assimilation of which the reformers had dreamed.

As James Comer has pointed out, the fact that black leaders were drawn largely from among those freedmen who had been in most direct contact with their masters and needed their approval and acceptance caused them to advance "the cause of the Negroes as a group most gingerly." Observing "the apathy, lack of achievement and asocial behavior of some of their fellows, many of them found their Negro identity a source of shame rather than psychological support. . . ."[13]

Lewis H. Blair, an aristocratic Virginian, labored as late as the 1880s to convince his fellow whites that the problem was "no less than the abandonment of the principle of separate schools, which principle is an efficient and certain mode of dooming to perpetual ignorance both whites and blacks in thinly settled sections."[14] Blair insisted that the only way to "peace, happiness, prosperity for all" was to assure the freed slaves of "the whole one hundred per cent" of their rights so that they might be "as free and as equal citizens as the proudest whites."[15]

But between the time of his treatise entitled *The Prosperity of the South Dependent upon the Elevation of the Negro* (1889) and the year 1916, Blair completely reversed himself on the racial issue. In an undated manuscript discovered after his death, Blair made, in C. Vann Woodward's words, "a complete and unqualified recantation of his equalitarian and liberal position of 1889 with regard to the Negro."[16] In doing so Blair only followed a path taken by a number of other whites

[13]James P. Comer, "The Social Power of the Negro," *Scientific American* 216 (April 1967), 4.
[14]Quoted in Lewis H. Blair, *Prophet without Honor*, C. Vann Woodward, ed., xxxviii.
[15]*Prophet without Honor*, xl.
[16]*Prophet without Honor*, xliv.

of the North and South alike. Blair remained liberal on most political issues, supporting Wilsonian progressivism to the end of his days. Like the Southern Populists, among whom Tom Watson was perhaps the most prominent, Blair abandoned his earlier hopes and declared that "the only logical position for the Negro is absolute subordination to the whites."[17]

Even more striking, however, was the change of mind reflected in many of the Negro leaders themselves. Martin Delany was one of the most active and able black leaders in the period prior to the Civil War and the first conspicuous black advocate of return of his people to Africa. Delany was a physician, a major in the United States Army, and an aide to Wade Hampton when the latter was postwar governor of South Carolina. Like his white counterpart, Lewis Blair, Delany came more and more to accept a subordinate position for the freed slave. The man who had fought with remarkable tenacity and skill to improve the condition of his people apparently became resigned to a dependent status for the race. As Theodore Draper has put it, "By the end of the century, few Negroes even had the right to vote in South Carolina. Delany seems to have had no regrets."[18]

Liberal historians, writing of Lewis Blair and others like him and of the era of Reconstruction generally, have almost uniformly attributed the increasing restrictions placed upon the freed slaves to a rising tide of white prejudice, what we today would call "a white backlash." According to this interpretation, Northern liberals and Southern reformers alike, having initially extended a helping hand to the freedman, suddenly drew back and abandoned their former wards to the most repressive and reactionary elements in the South. This argument of course has a lot to recommend it. There was unquestionably a withdrawal. Many individual Negroes had significant accomplishments to their credit, enough to give the lie to the theory that black people were inherently inferior. However, the great majority of these were former household slaves who had absorbed those white values and skills generally comprehended by the phrase "Protestant ethic." In the schools and colleges established by the reformers and in other philanthropic

[17]*Prophet without Honor*, xlv.
[18]*New York Review* 39, March 12, 1970.

enterprises, it proved impossible to *change the consciousness* of the great mass of freedmen. This was simply because the effort had, with the best of intentions, to be made from the outside.

The white reformer had no notion of the mental world of the black man, and under no circumstances could the guardians change the self-image of the wards. The self-image of the wards is in large part shaped by the guardians' image of them. *They are as the guardians see them.* Starting out with the assumption that there were no substantial or insurmountable differences in intellectual and social capacity between black and white, the reformers were dismayed to find that there were indeed very profound differences. They did not perceive these differences as differences of *consciousness* but, reluctantly, as innate differences. The utopian expectations of the reformers were defeated. Blacks proved far more resistant to being turned into whites than the reformers could have imagined.

From the perspective of the present, it is possible to see that (1) the blacks were victims of white stereotypes that even the most devoutly liberal whites could not entirely transcend and that the blacks themselves accepted in order to cope with white society and that (2) the blacks were fighting a desperately if largely subconscious battle to preserve their own identity. A people's consciousness, which under the proper circumstances can be transformed virtually overnight, is ordinarily most intractable. Reconstruction was an inadequate answer to an insolvable problem. By the middle of the seventies, the reaction against the freed slave had, one might say, become acute in proportion to the unrealistic expectations of this rapid transformation into a middle-class white consciousness within an incidentally black skin.

The suffering that black people endured as a result of disappointed liberal expectations may have been, in its psychological effect, more devastating to the race than the horrors of slavery, because blacks actually perceived the failure as at least in part their failure, a failure that seemed a confirmation of the views of those whites who saw blacks as irredeemably inferior. The result suggests the "double-bind"; white reformers could not face the implications of their defeat. The implication seemed to be that the black *was* biologically—and very substantially—inferior to the white, and that notion ran counter to the liberal Christian doctrine of redemption as the reformers of the nineteenth century understood that doctrine. No more could the implications of defeat be faced by blacks, the more articulate of whom attributed the failure of the Reconstruction to white prejudice and repression.

This view was given more than the color of truth by the fact that repression did take place. The repression, when it reached full tide, was rendered more harsh and bitter by the fact that those whites who had always considered the black race as markedly inferior to the white now turned savagely on the blacks, confirmed in their own prejudices by the failure of the contention that an end to involuntary servitude would progressively diminish the deep differences that racial determinists attributed to the innate capacities of the races. Such whites quite properly understood the profoundly unassimilated and deeply demoralized blacks to be a very serious threat to the white society which in many rural areas they far outnumbered. Repression, once initiated, seldom stops short of complete subordination and humiliation. That was the ironic fate of the freed slave: to descend into a darkness, in many ways more terrible than his servitude.

Out of that tragic prison of the soul, the black consciousness was to emerge, very truly "forged in the fires of adversity." But it emerged in its own way and in its own time, a time "of whom no man knows the hour of the fruit's ripening, for it ripens in a secret place and falls in its own time." This emerging has been a source of vast confusion and anxiety to white society; it was not ordained and planned by the guardians but, instead, found its own way, and this indeed is its most chastening and instructive lesson. It says to the dominant society: "There are events of the most profound significance that you, with all your marvelous technology, cannot anticipate, control or, *a posteriori*, understand."

In considering the requirements of "peoplehood," it is revealing to contrast the story of black people in America with those immigrant groups who arrived in the United States from the 1840s on. The Irish were, in a real sense, the first blacks. When they began to emigrate to America, victims of a series of famines, they were viewed in much the same way that the freed slaves were a generation later. The Irish were characterized as lazy, drunken, thieving, and immoral; they were relegated to the most dangerous and menial tasks. In the South they were often employed in jobs so unhealthy that slave owners did not wish to risk their slaves in the work. If an Irishman died, nothing was lost; a slave, on the other hand, represented a substantial investment.

However, if in the eyes of the established American the Irish immigrant appeared to have most of the deficiencies later ascribed to the freed slave, the Irishman certainly did not see himself in that light. He had a strong pride of race and nationality and social institutions of his own which were reasonably effective in protecting him against the most corrosive effects of prejudice—family, church, priest, clubs and associations, songs, poems, stories, even saloons. Far from accepting the natives' view of him, he regarded them with a cordial contempt and hatred, preserved by his sense of cultural identity. Above all, he had access to power through big-city political machines. He had a vote and he used it to pull himself out of the lower depths of American life. Moreover, while racial traits were evident in the Irish, they were in no wise so striking or ineradicable as with the black man. As James Comer has put it, "Immigrants voted, gained political influence, held public office, owned land and operated businesses. Group power and influence expanded individual opportunities and facilitated individual achievement, and within one or two generations most immigrants enjoyed the benefits of first-class American citizenship."[19]

The importance of common values and ideals, of a closely knit, highly integrated family, group, or community in the rise of its members, in their "vertical mobility" can hardly be overstated. It may be given as a general historical law that the capacity of individuals to ascend the social and economic scale in American society has been directly proportional to the coherence and intimacy of the groups to which they belonged. It is perhaps only out of the ghetto situation that members of oppressed minorities can find the psychological or moral resources to extricate themselves. The American Jewish ghetto, for example, was the most spectacular seedbed for the production of autonomous upwardly mobile individuals in our history (if one excepts the

---

[19]James P. Comer, "The Social Power of the Negro," *Scientific American* 216 (April 1967), 3.

Puritan communities of New England in some ways so much like them).

Here it is interesting to contrast the cases of the Irish and the Jews. The Irish created their own institutions—parochial schools, colleges, universities, even careers—most notably the three P's: priests, police, and politicians—all fashioned into an intricate subculture that protected them against the most corrosive effects of WASP prejudice. For the Jews the crucial point may have been the development of the Conservative and Reform branches of Judaism, which made vastly easier the assimilation of Jews into American life. The devices of the Irish were essentially conservative and protective; the tactics of the Jews were radical and aggressive. Their penetration of key areas of American business, mass entertainment, and intellectual life was astonishingly rapid and successful. Conservative and Reform Judaism turned out to contain exactly the right degree of adjustment to the American ethos while at the same time preserving virtually intact the most crucial aspects of Jewish cohesiveness, identity, and racial pride. If Jews, like Catholics, had been locked up within the confines of a rigid religious orthodoxy, their entry into American life would have been far slower and of a very different character.

The case of the Jews is clearly a special one. The story of Italians, Poles, Hungarians, and other Southern and Central European immigrants follows substantially the course of the Irish. Three other immigrant groups might be mentioned here: the Chinese, Japanese, and Mexicans. The three latter groups share with blacks (and American Indians) a distinctive skin color and physiognomy that clearly distinguishes them from the Anglo-Saxon type. The Japanese were a kind of Oriental Jew in that their religion, their family structure, and their general cultural background prepared them for a remarkably effective adjustment to American life. Notwithstanding the disgraceful episode of the World War II internment camps, their assimilation into their adopted country has been a notable success story. The fact is that internment camps had the effect, after the war, of speeding the assimilation of the Japanese because it forced them to realize how vulnerable their own cultural exclusiveness had made them. Their experience of the camps persuaded the Japanese that they must become Americans.

The situation of the Chinese was far more difficult. They were brought into the country as a form of indentured labor, and their case more closely resembles that of the early Irish immigrants. They proved relatively unassimilable in part because of their extreme exoticism and in part because they were drawn from the most depressed classes of China. Their racial distinctiveness was not matched by a disciplined and coherent sense of their own "identity." Their ghetto life was and remains primarily protective.

The Mexicans approached closely the situation of the Chinese with, of course, substantial differences. While the Chinese were urban and mercantile in temperament and thus readily formed racial ghettos, the Mexicans were basically agricultural workers dispersed on large farms and ranches as hired hands and seasonal labor. Moreover, they were to be found primarily in the Southwest and were thus an almost exclusively regional problem. At the same time, the proximity of their own country inhibited assimilation. They had a Spanish colonial cultural tradition that emphasized passivity and was rich in forms of consolation represented in the Catholic Church, an institution which verified and reinforced their differentness and discouraged efforts at assimilation.

Chinese, Mexican-Americans, and American Indians all share with American blacks a common "racial situation"; that is to say, they are identifiably different in facial characteristics and skin color from the dominant "whites." While this fact has undoubtedly contributed greatly to the repression and discrimination directed against them, the most important cultural common denominator among them is not their racial distinctiveness but the fact that they have all been, in one degree or another, wards of the dominant society, "masses" that could only be transformed into "people" by their ability to create their own consciousness.

Their problem has been complicated, of course, by the fact that in Western culture the freedom of a group from a subordinate, mass status has to do, in large part, with the concept of "the individual." People everywhere exist as members of groups, however nugatory and ill-defined, but the Western world has developed the concept of "the individual," and it is a concept unknown in many cultures. The individual was seen as a kind of autonomous unit, a complete being, self-validating, "the measure of all things." The individual has been for the Western imagination a most compelling idea, one that reached its epitome and embodiment in the American, the classic "inner-directed" man. The American vernacular is full of phrases that express this view: one individual is as good as another; all men are created equal; everyone has a right to "do his thing." One hears a constant litany, "the individual this or that"; the individual knows what is best for him; the individual must choose; and so on. In a society saturated with this ethic, it was inevitable that the needs and problems of the freed slave could not be dealt with or even understood.

While white society insisted on viewing the Negro as an individual, he struggled to develop a group or racial consciousness. As long as he was only an individual, he had only half an existence or half a reality. He could not become fully human until he was conscious of himself as "other," as Afro-American, or however he chose to define himself. The struggle to free himself from the enveloping, omnipresent consciousness of the white man and to achieve his own consciousness must certainly be one of the most poignant and dramatic episodes in history. As an individual, the black man was constantly at the mercy of the white man's tests, measures, and judgment.

Even the fact that the white society stated the issue in terms of equality prejudiced the outcome. The white liberal who insisted on the "equality" of the black man with the white did him almost as much a disservice as the reactionary who maintained that he was irredeemably inferior. The claim of "equality" for the black was a plainly ethnocentric judgment because it took the white as the unquestioned norm that the black was judged to be equal to. There was nothing in this liberal notion that took into account the fact that the black man might embody a different set of qualities and attributes that could not be comprehended by the word "equal" with its heavy freight of individuation. Moreover, the liberal argument ran in the face of all the direct evidence, which was that blacks were not equal. They were profoundly exotic and strikingly different. The white liberals' faith in equality played into the hands of the out-and-out racist who observed more accurately that the black was not equal, which meant for the racist that he was inferior. Much of this confusion arose out of the American determination to see human beings as individuals rather than as members of groups—families, congregations, clans, castes, communities.

Ironically, while the freed slave could only be seen as an "individual," the category of "black" in which the white man had placed the slave had no meaning for the black himself. The black man in Africa was an Ibo, a Yoruba, a Masai. He did not identify himself as an African any more than a French peasant thought of himself as a European. His sense of racial unity was quite simply forced on him by the white who, in stripping the black man of his tribal identity, imposed a spurious identity on him. The case was almost identical with the American Indian who again was tribal and had no concept of himself as "an Indian." He, like the African black, was a Cherokee, a Pequot, a Seminole, or a Huron with a fierce pride in his tribe. A Shawnee or a Choctaw was observed by the white man as an Indian. Even more clearly than the blacks, the Indians represent the relationship of wards to their guardian. The Indians, simply by virtue of being forced to refrain from waging war, an activity on which most of the tribal cultures rested, were deprived of their identity. The whites could not tolerate Indians as warring, hunting, nomadic tribes and the Indians could not survive psychologically on reservations. They became, in consequence, the pathetic and perpetual wards of the United States government in one of the most extreme instances of alienation in modern history.

The tribal divisions of the Indians were perpetuated by their location on reservations. They retained just enough of their tribal life to prevent any significant assimilation of white culture. One of the striking consequences of the black power movement is the stirring of representatives of various tribes to a concerted if still modest effort to escape from their status as wards.

Unlike the Indians and the blacks, the immigrants, while experiencing initially gross forms of prejudice, made their way comparatively rapidly into the mainstream of American life, readily adopting the American ethic of individualism. They took pride in the way in which, in their view, they had by *individual* efforts struggled up from the lower depths of American society to comfortable positions in the lower middle, the middle, and the upper class. Not understanding the crucial importance of their own cultural, social, and even in a sense political institutions in that achievement, immigrants have looked with hostility and contempt on blacks for not having emulated their upward mobility.

From slavery, to Reconstruction, to black power—blacks in America are creating their own "black consciousness" with profound effects on other minority groups and on black people all over the world. What the shape and content of that black consciousness will be when it has taken clearer form no one can presently say with any certainty. But all revolutions must ultimately make their peace with the old order, in this case the order of the white society, which is, in any event, a major component of black consciousness. That which is initially rejected must be finally taken back, but taken back, of course, in a form very much altered by all the intervening events. Whatever else may be obscure, it is entirely clear at this point that the "invisible man" has become dramatically visible.

The nature of black consciousnesss may still be problematical, but the white man's *consciousness of the black* has already been radically altered. He may be sympathetic, fearful, or profoundly hostile, but wherever he looks he *sees the new black man*, often with "natural" hair, a striking beard or moustache, a bizarre costume. The black man's deep sense of drama (which is doubtless the consequence of playing a dozen different roles on which his survival often quite literally depended) is now employed to astonish and alarm the white. One has the sense that the Panthers are, in a curious way, actors in an often bloody drama, designated primarily to terrify whites. The matter is, of course, more complicated, but it is necessary to emphasize the significance of "acting" in the theatrical sense for dependent and subordinate groups.

When John Adams heard of the Boston Tea Party, he perceived at once the dramatic significance of the act and wrote in his journal, "This is the most magnificent moment of all. There is a dignity, a majesty, a sublimity, in this last effort of the patriots, that I greatly admire. The people should never rise without doing something to be remembered—something notable and striking. This destruction of the tea is so bold, so daring, so firm, intrepid and inflexible and it must have so important consequences, and so lasting, that I can't but consider it an epoch in history."[20] In a contemporary phrase, the Boston Tea Party was America's most spectacular performance of "guerrilla theatre."

Such drama is not enacted merely to frighten the dominant group and alter its consciousness of the dependent group. It is therapeutic for the actors; it strengthens them in their encounters with representatives of the dominant groups. When Black Panthers defy the police, call them pigs, and even on occasion bring on shoot-outs, most black people, however they may repudiate such behavior, feel in their hearts that they themselves have gained a substantial measure of power and self-confidence in dealing with figures that they may have always feared. This is certainly one of the classic functions of dramatic art—to heighten our awareness of our own powers and capacities.

This is why such behavior is never, in the strictest sense, revolutionary. It requires an audience and when the audience leaves the theatre the actors go home to their everyday concerns or to write the scenario for the next performance. To describe the Black Panthers in this way is not to diminish their importance or to treat lightly the very real and serious consequences of their dramas, particularly, of course, for themselves. All their lives most black people take pains to stay out of the way of police who are, for them, the symbol and fact of harassment and repression. That is why the Black Panthers feel they must seek out the police and strip them of their fearfulness. They must make the police *fear blacks*.

Members of predominantly white audiences have heard black speakers denounce all whites and in the most unsparing terms only to be told subsequently that they shouldn't really take the imprecations to heart, that they were not meant "personally," just as in watching a play, however much one may be moved by the words of the actors, one does not believe them to be "real." Drama has always had in part the function of providing a cover for changing understandings and relationships within a society. For this change to take place it is necessary that all factions and parties be represented in the audience, otherwise the drama loses much of its effect. Only the egoist seeking self-confirmation enjoys preaching to the converted. An audience is not a revolution; by

[20]*Diary and Autobiography of John Adams*, vol. 2 (1771–1781), L. H. Butterfield, ed., *The Adams Papers* (Cambridge, Mass.: Belknap Press, 1961), 85–86.

virtue of accepting the conventions of the theatre, it listens to things that it could not listen to in another context, without going to war, committing murder, or seeking escape in suicide.

Every age of revolutionary change—or, more accurately, every episode of revolutionary change—has in it this demonic, possessed, obscene, irrational element. It is there because the members of the dependent group are enacting terrifying new rituals that are designed to strengthen them in their confrontation with the dominant culture. Rational argument and naive goodwill never prove effective in changing the world. The world is changed by passion. The dependent group has to expiate its ingratitude by hating its guardians, albeit that hate is often ritualized and symbolic. The dependent group, moreover, is not essentially revolutionary in its aims because it wishes to come into the inheritance of the dominant group, not to destroy that inheritance.

Peoplehood is a particular kind of self-definition whereby masses or wards of the public seek to achieve an identity and a power of their own. This is essential to emphasize because the definition always comes out of the mass; it can never come from the outside, from well-intentioned liberals, benefactors, reformers, philosophers, psychologists, sociologists; all are equally impotent in the face of such a world historical event. All are equally surprised and confounded. All rush desperately to keep up, to explain what is happening and why, and what will surely happen next, and almost before their explanations have been formulated and printed in the latest journal, a new turn of events, a new effusion, a new passionate outpouring has made them obsolete, irrelevant, erroneous.

The dependent group in the process of defining itself, or creating itself, of speaking itself into life, draws on remarkable new sources of energy and releases these into the world. One is indeed tempted to use a mechanical model and to speak of this process as though the emerging group had actual access to some new source of energy, to some electrifying force. They become electrified, plugged in, almost literally, to history. They sense that they, too, can make history. Individuals who could not conceivably have commanded our attention—who did not have the power—achieve the power. And this, of course, is why a figure like Malcolm X is such a crucial figure to the black community. He found and tapped that great source of power. Women, in the beginning of their struggle for equality, tapped the same source of power.

The dependent group disciplines itself. Of course, the most conspicuous instance here would be the very strict discipline down to matters of dress and personal morality of a group like the Black Muslims. Many women in the period from 1840 to 1930 renounced the conventional roles of wife and mother because they thought that the struggle that they had entered was of such critical importance that it was necessary for them to do so.

As a consequence of this discipline, the leaders of masses emerging into peoplehood are able to achieve remarkable things that ordinary mortals seldom achieve, because the leaders of the masses *are filled with history*, with the ecstasy of a sense of destiny. They not only suffer terrible strains and pressures as a consequence, they suffer them, for the most part, like soldiers, like heroes, and with a strange kind of exaltation. Groups emerging into peoplehood have other minor but interesting similarities. Their leaders wear distinctive costumes; that is a crucial aspect of their enterprise. For blacks the dashiki has been an example. For women it was the costume (not developed by Amelia Bloomer, as a matter of fact, although it had her name) that consisted of slacks and a little jacket. It was a very modest costume, but it was immediately attacked as a most scandalous and obscene costume, sure to undermine morality and destroy the American home.

Violence, of course, is a major part of the shock therapy of the wards. The violence is almost invariably symbolic and is the cause of considerable anguish on the part of those liberal advocates of the dependent groups who are not themselves members of these groups. They debate endlessly the question of whether violence, which is itself so basically unjust, so heedless of the rights and often the lives of the innocent, is ever justified. This issue was a constant bone of contention between John and Sam Adams and it was the central issue in one of the most dramatic trials in American history, that in which John Adams defended the British soldiers for firing on a threatening mob at the occasion of the Boston Massacre. The soldiers were for all practical purposes acquitted, and Adams's reputation for the moment passed under a cloud. But Adams dramatized the point that the cause of justice must not proceed by injustice, or that the injustice (the violence) if deemed essential to the cause should be measured out as scrupulously and precisely as if on an apothecary's scale. The patriot effort after the Boston Massacre to make the soldiers the victims of what was in fact a riot was going too far; the Boston Tea Party, on the other hand, was exactly right—dramatic, decisive, and above all causing no loss of life.

The leaders of the dependent group argue, with perhaps irrefutable logic, that violence, especially against property, is a crucial tactic in awakening the dominant group to the real situation and to the real needs of the dependent class. This is true especially in a modern capitalist society where property is, in a degree, sacred and where the destruction of television sets, or banks, is viewed by some people as more serious than the loss of human life. While it can be said that violence directed towards property is an extreme and dangerous tactic, it is at the same time a highly effective and perhaps indispensable tactic at a certain stage of the struggle of subordinate and dependent groups to change their status in relation to the dominant society. Violence directed towards persons (outside of the occasions of demonstrations and riots) is the ultimate revolutionary weapon and represents a threat to society that society must meet with whatever resources are available to it.

There are conspicuous sexual elements in all these upheavals. It is most evident in the Women's Rights Movement in the issues of prostitution, free love, contraception, divorce. But it is evident too in the Black Revolution, in white fantasies about black sexuality and in the issue of miscegenation. In these strange upheavals whereby masses become people, we see certain common traits: passionate speech (and ranting), eccentric and symbolic dress, almost military discipline, violence, and pronounced sexual aspects. We observe consciousness transformed and vast new energies released in society. We witness a process, in theological terms, of redemption; an event, or in this case a series of events, of profound significance, unpredictable, whereby masses achieve peoplehood out of their own inner resources, out of the fires of their spirit, against all the odds, out of dependence and subordination, out of the depths of degradation in the case of blacks. These events belong to a class of the most touching and dramatic episodes in history. They are truly inspired. They dramatize people's capacity for transcendence. Because they are never "caused" in any explicit way, and thus can never truly be "explained," they press upon our attention the profound regenerative forces in humanity that are the best hope for the future of the race.

The Lessons

1983 of American History

Lord Bolingbroke, the eighteenth-century English politician (and others before him), described history as "philosophy teaching by example," and historians over the subsequent generations have debated the lessons history taught and indeed whether it taught any lessons at all. It is my settled conviction, of course, that history does indeed teach lessons: I am here concerned with the lessons of American history.

First, I should make clear certain basic assumptions about the nature of the historical process itself; the history of the race of which the history of the United States is a subdivision. I understand history to be a tragic drama, tragic in the sense that individuals and peoples die, that all things are transitory, that we do not know with certainty why we are here, how we got here, and what our destiny is. We perceive life as through a glass, darkly. It is given to us only to have intimations. So we live by faith. History is, moreover, full of tragedies of our own doing, of war, oppression, violent death, and acute suffering, in addition to the calamities of nature. So it does not seem to me excessively pessimistic to call history a "tragic" drama. Now the only reason we can bear to live at all, I suspect, is that history (life) is a "drama," that our lives individually and collectively are full of drama of the highest order, the simplest lives as well as the most famous. The most awesome evidence of the profoundly dramatic character of life is, of course, art. Art is mind and imagination recording and enhancing that dramatic quality of life that saves us from immobilizing despair. Since history is coterminous with life, is nothing but life, it must be congruent with life. We cannot, and this is part of our tragedy, understand life, that is, history. If we could understand life, we could of course understand history and vice versa. Since we cannot understand history or life in any final or comprehensive way, historians have the primary obligation *to tell what happened*. Of course, we can't even do that very well. We can only hint at the remarkable complexity and inexhaustible drama, the breathtaking richness and variety of the experiences of people in history. And in this account of what happened, this inadequate narrative, we have to keep several things in mind: first, of course, that we cannot tell it as fully as it merits; we cannot, more explicitly, exceed the limits of art. In addition, we must keep in mind that, as Thomas Carlyle put it, history is the sum of innumerable biographies. Of these innumerable biographies, we can only tell a few. Only a few are of course recoverable, but of those that are, we can only recount a fraction, so that fraction had better represent as fairly and fully as possible the whole range of a people's lives in the segment of time the historian has chosen to reflect upon. This cannot be too much emphasized. Without the feeling of real lives, deeply lived, there can, in my opinion, be no real history, whatever you may call it. Without the sense of lives lived, the inherent drama of history is lost; no drama, no history. This is not, needless to say, the attitude of academic historians; they hold to quite the reverse, for they have the touching notion that history is some kind of thing called a social science and that their obligation as some kind of scientist is to be as detached, objective, and impersonal as possible (and that, may I say, is not very "detached, objective, and impersonal"). So history is first of all about lives, individuals, people, men, women, and children, tycoons and farmers, workers and poets and painters and professors, exploiters and reformers. There are no "blind forces," there is no "dialectic," there are no "laws of historical development" except in a very limited and rudimentary sense, no teleology, no automatic progress, no evolutionary *process* (although, as I shall argue later, there is progress of a kind, limited and contingent as it may be). This means that the most important quality of the historian is a willingness to listen to the authentic voices of those who have preceded us. What they said has more power by far than what the historians may come to say about what they said. They are the essential materials of history—what people thought and equally what they felt, their dreams and aspirations and anxieties and fears. There is no eloquence, Charles Francis Adams the first wrote, like the eloquence of facts. "Our passions give life to the world; our collective passions constitute the history of mankind," Rosenstock-Huessy added.

Finally, history is permeated by morality. Great crimes are committed in history that it would be absurd to call by any other name. The essence of our tragic drama is the conflict between good and evil. And yet we must temper judgment with compassion and an understanding of the historical context in which our characters lived (thus it is silly and jejune to denounce Washington or Jefferson for having slaves).

These are all generalizations about the nature of history itself and I have promised, after all, to talk about the lessons of American history, but I trust this is not time wasted. I believe it is intellectually irresponsible to undertake to write history without having taken the trouble to try at least to come to some reasonably clear conclusions about its overall form and nature. If the historian fails to do this, I do not see how he can be entirely honest with his readers because he is always, in a sense, arguing from unstated assumptions.

We might begin our consideration of American history with John Calvin's *Institutes of the Christian Religion* because the Protestant Reformation was the essential precondition of British colonial America, but John Winthrop's *Modell of Christian Charity* will do as well.

On board the *Arbella* on his way to Massachusetts Bay, Winthrop, the leader of the great Puritan migration, wrote out an intellectual and spiritual charter for this daring new venture. He and his fellow Puritans had set out to form a new kind of human community or, at least, one that looked for its inspiration back to the faithful communities of the primitive Christian church. They were to share each other's burdens, to care for each other in want or illness, to be, indeed, like the ligaments of a single body—"to do justly, to love mercy, to walk humbly with our God." But more than that they were to be as "a city upon a hill," a model of Christian charity, an example for those who followed them and indeed for those who remained at home as well, a beacon for the weary and the heavy-laden.

So the original and most basic aspiration was to reform the world, to make it a great Christian commonwealth.

By the middle of the eighteenth century, the British colonists had become a new kind of person. They were no longer willing to be dependent and subordinate people subject to the whims, as it seemed to them at least, of a remote king and privy council. They were thus ready to launch the first revolt in modern times of a colonial people against their rulers. When they did this the colonists took their place in a succession of modern revolutions, the first of which had been the English Civil War, led by Parliament and, eventually, Cromwell, on behalf of the rights of the people as opposed to the arbitrary acts of a discredited monarch, and concluded by the so-called Glorious Revolution. From having started out as simple resistance to an arbitrary act—specifically the Stamp Act—the American Revolution discovered new political and social principles—no hereditary class structure, a kind of theoretical equality between people, submission to natural law, federalism, republican government, and, reluctantly, democracy.

Now the "consciousness" of the men who codified these notions in two crucial documents, the Declaration and the Constitution, was what I have called the Classical-Christian Consciousness. It was distinguished by an essentially pessimistic (or realistic) view of human nature shared by Greek and Christian cultures—Aristotle wrote, "Man is a pig"; the prophet Jeremiah declared, "The heart of man is desperately wicked and deceitful." With a deep suspicion of power (and the conviction that, unchecked, it was always in the long run abused), the Classical-Christian Consciousness believed that at the same time there was a "natural" and moral order in the universe (ordained by God, in the Christian view) that it was man's duty to try to discover and, once having discovered, to try to live by, however imperfectly.

At the same time, the Founding Fathers, the Framers, as men of their time, were deeply affected by the intellectual currents of the so-called Enlightenment, which held, in brief, that man was good, rational, and, in time, perfectable—a translation of the Christian heaven to earth ("the voice of the people is the voice of God"). While the Founding Fathers, with certain notable exceptions, *did not* believe this, they half believed it. They shared the Enlightenment faith in education and its suspicion of the intrusion of the church into the state and vice versa. They also partook of what the British critic Wyndham Lewis called "radical universalism." They believed that mankind was somewhat rational and everywhere oppressed by kings, tyrants, and aristocrats; that people, if not "good" (if, indeed, tainted by original sin), nonetheless aspired to freedom and were capable, with responsible leadership, of governing themselves. This was the "revolutionary" part of the American Revolution. It wished by precept to strike the chains off the oppressed of the world. The French Revolution seemed both a confirmation and extension of the American Revolution. Out of it came the Secular-Democratic Consciousness. The Reverend Samuel Thatcher in a Fourth of July address in Concord, Massachusetts, in 1796, expressed this sentiment eloquently. "All Hail! Approaching Revolutions," he exclaimed. "Americans have lived ages in a day." We met to celebrate the "consequent emancipation of a world."

So that is one essential lesson: the rejection of subordination and dependence broadening out into a call for the emancipation of the oppressed of the world in the name of self-government.

The second essential lesson is less inspiring. It is, of course, that these professions were fatally flawed by slavery and that the nation, in a certain sense, could not begin until that tragic paradox was resolved: a substantial portion of the inhabitants of the United States were not free at all; they were slaves, and slaves, moreover, under the most terrible and degrading circumstances imaginable.

Most Americans were willing, for a wide variety of reasons, to accept slavery as a "given," something regrettable but something about which nothing could be done. They wished to bury it in the most remote recesses of their consciousness. But Benjamin Lundy would not let them. Soon others, equally adamant, joined Lundy (in the first year of its life, his *Genius of Universal Emancipation* had only ten subscribers), among them William Lloyd Garrison. Slowly, painfully, year by year they grew into a goodly company, the emancipators, the antislavery gang, the abolitionists. They would not let their fellow-Americans rest in their un-Christian subjection of fellow human beings. They preached day and night that all men were brothers. The Bible said so. Slavery was not merely "a peculiar social institution," it was a grievous sin, an offense to the Lord, a mockery of all America's pretensions to be "the land of the free." How could there be a land of the free that enslaved another race?

So there was a war provoked, in the main, by those voices that would not be silent and could not, in the long run, be borne. A terrible war was fought to preserve the union and free the slaves. The country could begin. James Russell Lowell wrote that at last he could love his country, fully and without shame. So that is an enormous "meaning," a meaning of inexhaustible potency. It places the issue of slavery and the crusade of the abolitionists against it at the center of our history; everything else is secondary.

It turned out, as we know, that the situation of black people in America was far from resolved. The ex-slaves and blacks in other parts of the United States were subjected to terrible indignities and the condition of many of them came to be, objectively, worse in so-called freedom than in slavery.

The next overriding fact was what was called for sixty years or so "the war between capital and labor." The word "war" is an accurate description of the perpetual and bitter struggle of working men and women for decent wages and decent conditions of labor. In 1877, the most dramatic episode in this war took place, a spontaneous general strike that began in western Maryland with workers on the B & O and spread to virtually every major industrial city in the country. For over a week many of the nation's railroads were tied up. National Guard and federal troops along with thousands of hastily deputized citizens were called out to try to restore order. In Pittsburgh alone, over 3,500 railroad cars were destroyed by protesting strikers.

Chicago was virtually paralyzed for days. Many Americans feared that the revolution predicted by Karl Marx had started.

John Swinton, who edited a labor magazine, reflected that the Great Strikes were the most dangerous and destructive episode in the United States between the end of the Civil War and the end of the century, a period of thirty-five years.

Henry George wrote *Progress and Poverty* in the aftermath of the Great Strikes, and legions of reformers took up the cause of immigrants and working men and women in the following decades, until they constituted as bold and active an army as the abolitionists. Many, like Wendell Phillips, had been leaders of the abolition movement, many others, like Jane Addams, were the sons and daughters of abolitionists. So the spirit of the abolitionists continued to manifest itself as the most powerful force for reform in the nation.

Millions of Americans, horrified by the cruelty and oppression that came in the wake of industrial capitalism, became active or nominal socialists. There were working-class socialists, upper-class and middle-class socialists, syndicalists, Christian socialists, and Marxist socialists, not to mention a generous helping of anarchists and synco-anarchists. Conservative Brooks Adams wrote a book in 1913 called *A Theory of Social Revolution* in which he argued that no class or group that had held power in any epoch of history had ever willingly surrendered it or shared it in response to pressure from the less fortunate, more accurately, the exploited. On that basis he predicted a revolution in the United States.

Whether reformers or revolutionists would have won out is impossible to say with complete confidence. Certainly the reformers, stimulated by Rooseveltian Progressivism, were beginning to make substantial inroads on the power of the capitalists. Moreover, Woodrow Wilson, elected President in 1912, began immediately to carry out important reforms.

So the war between capital and labor was the central fact of the post-Civil War period.

But there was another enormously important and closely related development—the great flood of immigration from eastern and southern Europe that poured into the United States between 1890 and 1913 (it was only terminated by the war). It rose to 1,285,349 in 1907. As important as the numbers were the places of origin. Most of these were new. They included immigrants from "peoples" if not races that most Americans had never even heard of—Ruthenians, Magyars, Montenegrins, Serbs, Bohemians, Dalmatians, Bosnians, Herzegovinians, Croatians.

Almost nine million came in the decade 1901–1910, substantially more than twice as many as came in the preceding decade and as many as in the period from 1881 to 1901. By 1910, there were over thirteen million foreign-born persons living in the United States. Immigration was far from a new story in America as we know, but the volume of immigrants and their antecedents were new elements in our history. When there was a strike of the textile mills in Paterson, New Jersey, the strikers spoke twenty-seven languages.

It was rather as though the roster of the peoples of the world was being somehow completed in the United States so that we would in fact be the first universal state in history.

To be the refuge and resort of such a variety of the human race is certainly unprecedented for a particular nation. It is a fact of such extraordinary potency that our imaginations fall far short of discerning the meaning. It caused extreme xenophobia among the earlier arrivals; indeed, panic and hysteria would not be too strong a description of their emotions.

Now, just at the moment when this vast movement of variegated humanity was at its full tide, the European war broke out. The psychological effects of this catastrophe among the millions of recent immigrants were, needless to say, extreme. Many had planned to go home and now found it difficult to do so. Others, who had not yet become naturalized American citizens, were summoned home to serve in the armed forces of the nation from which they had come. Complicating the situation was the fact that many of the immigrants were from the Austro-Hungarian empire and were involved with "liberation movements" within that empire—Bosnians, Serbs, Slavs, Slovaks, and Montenegrins among them. Did they owe their alliance to the United States (which had, on the whole, treated them very badly), or to the Austro-Hungarian Empire, or to "freeing" Bosnia or Bohemia from "foreign rule"?

The long delay (so-called American neutrality, which turned out to be increasingly unneutral) increased anxieties and encouraged the hope that the United States might remain out of the war entirely. Our entry into the war after so many pious avowals of our determination not to was especially traumatic for those immigrants who identified with the Central Powers.

When the war was over, the forces of reform, liberal or radical, seemed shattered beyond repair. There was, it turned out, a new enemy, "Godless" communist Russia, and every voice that spoke for reform in the United States was charged with being an agent of Godless communist Russia. The United States became paralyzed by its fear of "Red" revolution.

The depression of 1932 was, in large part, the economic consequence of the Peace of Versailles in which, out of fear and greed in almost equal parts, the victors destroyed the economy of Europe.

In the United States, the Great Depression turned out to be in some ways a blessing in disguise. It broke the spirit and the resistance of capitalism to widespread social reform. Such reforms, it seems clear, could never have been pushed through Congress in "good times." As it was, the demoralized capitalists could put up only a token opposition. Their collective voice sunk to gloomy mutterings. At long last it was possible to make peace in the sixty-year-long war between capital and labor. The second great conflict in our history was finally resolved (of course it created problems of its own in time). First slavery was abolished; then labor was given a "fair share" of the bounty or booty of capital.

So there has been not so much progress perhaps but redemption. Redemption from our most deplorable sins. We have a larger, more humane view of our responsibilities toward each other. We have jettisoned a considerable baggage of outmoded and unjust notions about society and our fellows. We have chastened if not tamed capital. But beyond all these things (and far more significant, I suspect, in the long run), we have somehow, in all this agony and desperate struggle produced, to use Wyndham Lewis's phrase, the "cosmic man." We have managed not only a reconciliation of capital and labor but of nations and peoples. The fact that the peoples of central and southern Europe had filled up the roster in the decades immediately preceding the World War was very largely responsible for those same peoples achieving their separate identities in the Versailles Treaty. The Treaty did not draw lines and divide peoples with exactly the wisdom of Solomon but it did take a long and remarkable step toward the ideal, given its most dramatic representation by the American Revolution, that "peoples," identifiable social or cultural and racial units, should be free to work out their own destinies; clearly this process continues with the incorporation of millions of Spanish-speaking peoples of Central and South America.

So what then are the lessons of American history? First the passion to redeem the world. Then the refusal to be dependent and subordinate — the first colonial revolt in other words; then the determination to turn this revolt into a genuine revolution by establishing the principle of self-government and abolishing all formal class distinctions. Next the validation of this principle by preserving the union and freeing the slaves, demonstrating in the process that it takes at least two generations of devoted labor to eradicate a serious social injustice. Further, providing a refuge, even while exploiting millions of the surplus or marginal populations of the Old World, thereby making possible the liberation of the corresponding peoples of the Old World who constituted "free constituencies" in the New. Finally, making peace, with the aid of the Great Depression, in the war between capital and labor.

Part Two
Education

The Sins

1954 of Higher
Education

In 1909 Woodrow Wilson gave an address during the inauguration of Ernest Fox Nichols as president of Dartmouth College, in the course of which he remarked that the effort to formalize the relationship between teacher and pupil in the interest of greater efficiency and larger bodies of students had led to pedagogy, the study of teaching techniques, and in proportion as we make teaching a science we separate ourselves from the vital processes of life. He said:

A College represents a passion, a very handsome passion, to which we should seek to give greater and greater force as the generations go by—a passion . . . for the things which live, for the things which enlighten, for the things which bind men together in unselfish companies.

Wilson was sure that

we shall never succeed in creating this organic passion, this great use of the mind. . . until [we] have utterly destroyed the practice of merely formal contact . . . between teacher and pupil.[1]

It is hard to add anything to this analysis of our educational ills, made in 1909. Certainly, nothing has happened since then to meet Woodrow Wilson's criticism of higher education. Formalism is the rule more than ever before, and our colleges are conspicuously without passion "for the things which enlighten, for the things which bind men together in unselfish companies." We have succumbed to mass education and even

[1] "The American College," reprinted in J. M. O'Neill, *Modern Short Speeches* (New York: Century Company, 1925), 202–207. Quotations from pages 203 and 205.

presume to call it an achievement. Students in our large colleges and universities are receptors, passive note takers, repeaters of ritual formulas, objects. They are voiceless. Rosenstock-Huessy has offered as an educational axiom, *respondeo itsi mutabor* ("I answer that I may change"). But the student today does not answer and therefore cannot change. To answer, a student needs not an examination paper but a respondent, someone who speaks to him by name, with whom he carries on a dialogue. The symbol of the bleak impersonality of our universities is the marking system. The papers of the students are frequently not even marked by the professor but by an assistant, so stereotyped has the learning process become.

Let me describe a typical university classroom. It is a large hall in which are gathered from fifty to four hundred students. The professor walks into the room; spreads out his lecture notes, which, the students do not fail to observe, are frequently yellow with age; talks, often not especially well, for fifty minutes; and then walks out. In order for the student in the large sophomore and freshman classes to have a lively and stimulating contact with a teacher—a chance to answer back—the classes are often divided into "quiz sections" of twenty-five to fifty students under the care of a teaching assistant. This is invariably a harassed graduate student of little experience, whose principal concern is not with his students but with finishing his degree requirements as quickly as possible and getting a job. Moreover, however diligent and devoted the teaching assistant may be, his lack of experience is a serious handicap, and the conditions under which he works are not conducive to effective teaching. Indeed, there would be more logic in having the teaching assistants give the lectures, which can be prepared from standard and readily available sources, while the professors met with the smaller sections for discussion and debate, but the professor is not likely to propose such a plan himself. The lecture provides a minimal means of discharging the formal responsibility of the professor to the student, and this, it might as well be admitted, is the aim of many professors. Indeed, I have heard some of my colleagues boast about their dexterity in avoiding students by having office hours at inconvenient times or in inaccessible places.

Why should the professor be so anxious to fulfill his formal responsibilities in the narrowest and most limited way? Simply because he must protect his time for "original research." What is the original research which the professor must perform? Frequently it is a grubby little monograph on some obscure point that is of no general interest, written without skill or wit, published in a small, money-losing edition, to secure a promotion. Or it may be an even more obscure article in a learned journal, which will count so many points toward the next advancement up the academic ladder. That a third- or fourth-rate piece of "scholarship" will win promotion far more quickly than first-rate teaching is another truism of the profession. It must be said to the glory of what is perhaps our greatest university that some departments have brilliant teachers, promoted, respected, and immensely effective, whose scholarly output would not be sufficient to procure their promotion at West Podunk Normal.

As a result of this elevation of "original research" into an academic god, the whole level of American scholarly output has been depressed. Piles of pedestrian work are turned out year after year by drudging scholars, and this vast tide flows over the academic world, leaving it largely unmarked. Teaching, which some heretical voice occasionally suggests is the principal function of the teacher, inevitably suffers from being treated as a matter of secondary or tertiary importance, and since teaching even of a superior quality is given little more than lip service as a basis for promotion in most universities, teachers with some sense of dedication are disheartened by the feeling that their talents are lightly regarded and poorly rewarded. Moreover, the pressure on young faculty members to publish promptly in order to attract favorable attention and win quick promotion is hardly compatible with the slow maturing of their talents or with the kind of ambitious, long-range projects that would take many years to complete but be ultimately of far more importance than a yearly output of trivia.

The college and university teacher unquestionably suffers nervous strain and anxiety from the present preposterous emphasis on publication. The defenders of the system offer two principal arguments in its support. First, that universities especially, but colleges too, are centers of learning. Thus an important part of their service to the intellectual community is to add to the sum of human knowledge. Second, continuing research is essential if a professor is to remain abreast of the latest developments in the field and be a vigorous and lively teacher.

The first argument is based on the very doubtful proposition that knowledge in the humanities and social sciences is cumulative, that more and more monographs on Shakespeare's rhetoric or the incidence of diphtheria in the French provinces in the seventeenth century will inevitably give us a deeper understanding of Shakespeare's greatness or of seventeenth-century France. The fact is that only when such studies are done with discernment, imagination, and true insight—are, in other words, to a degree inspired—will they add anything to anything.

The second point is perhaps even more fallacious. Every student has known monumental scholars who were the most deadly lecturers and teachers imaginable. Conversely, many of the most accomplished teachers whom I have encountered in my academic career did little "original research." If a man is a dedicated teacher, he will always seek to refresh his mind and his spirit, and he will generally do it by a catholicity of interest that is the very antithesis of narrow specialization. On the other hand, if he is not a good teacher, "original research" certainly will not make him one.

The principal sufferer from our existing canons of scholarship in universities and colleges is, of course, the student. In the large universities, the vast majority of the students pass through four years without having a fruitful contact with any professor, often without indeed having a professor once call them by name. They are like the audience in a darkened movie house, watching the screen, anonymous and indistinguishable. When I was a teaching assistant at Harvard, I spent a good deal of time, although only a lowly graduate student, writing letters of recommendation for honors graduates of the university who in four years of college knew not one of the eminent men who graced the faculty, but only me and perhaps several other academic underlings. Now this is not merely an unfortunate situation to be generally deplored. It is intellectually immoral and entirely hostile to that true education for which Woodrow Wilson raised his voice in 1909. The college student today is instructed, not taught. There is a kind of symbolic significance in the fact that while at most universities we are carefully subdivided into assistant, associate, and full professors, we are all lumped under the generic term "instructors." We inform the students, but we take no responsibility for what has been the historic task of the teacher, to "form" them. We are the victims of our misguided reverence for "the facts," when we should know that there are no facts, no comforting ultimate entities, at least on this earth, but rather hypotheses, conjectures, theses which may throw a flickering light on the human predicament. While we give lip service to the currently fashionable doctrines of pragmatism and relativism, most of us teach as though the important points had been pretty well settled, and our reliance on textbooks is the best indication of this abdication to the "established facts," or the "latest theory."

Of course many students welcome this. They accept quite readily the contractual nature of modern higher education. The unwritten contract between student and teacher goes something like this: the student is given material in lectures and textbooks that he is expected to memorize. He may, in some instances, be encouraged to question it, but first he must memorize it. Then, to the degree that he remembers the material and records it on an examination, he is rewarded by a mark. The student who works hardest and memorizes the most generally gets the best mark, and so on down the line. Everything thus comes to revolve around the marking system. In the bureaucracy of the modern university, the mark represents the only assessment of the student's capacity, and it measures an absurdly narrow range of abilities and responses. It follows that marks are, therefore, of great importance to the student. His scholarship, his teaching credentials, his draft status, his job—all are influenced by his marks. This means a thoroughly unhealthy emphasis on them, while at best they should be only a minor means to the major end of education; yet they inevitably become for the student an end in themselves. Alfred North Whitehead warned some years ago that

> our modes of testing ability will exclude all the youth whose ways of thought lie outside our conventions of learning. In such ways the universities, with their scheme of orthodoxies, will stifle the progress of the race unless by some fortunate stirring of humanity, they are in time remodeled or swept away.[2]

[2]*Essays in Science and Philosophy* (New York: Philosophical Library, 1947), 26.

The marking system is the bulwark of our "scheme of orthodoxies." Generally it does not occur to the student to question the morality or humanity of this system. He often cheats (at one large university 50 percent of the undergraduates who answered a questionnaire on the subject stated that they cheated from time to time) because he has no respect for the integrity of such a system. There is no reason, as far as I can see, why he should. The system has only a spurious integrity at best.

It is a fact of tragic dimensions that the most terribly depersonalized part of our depersonalized society is the college and university campus. Education takes place where minds come into close and vital contact; the passive note takers in college lecture courses do not fulfill this requirement. Education is not a process of transmitting often obsolete information; it is a matter of transmitting inspiration, not of instructing but of awakening and, ultimately, of transforming. Education is not a body of facts, but a habit of mind. It is fairly obvious that no large proportion of American college students are acquiring those habits of mind that should be the intellectual reflexes of the educated man or woman.

I do not, of course, mean to imply that the spiritual and intellectual sterility of our colleges and universities is due to the inhumanity of the people who administer them and teach in them. No more would I attribute the shortcomings of the primary and secondary schools to the perverseness of the intelligent and dedicated people who set their standards. The fact is that the educational theories on which American school and college education are based have been derived from the same views of the world and of man's relation to it.

This metaphysic has many branches and many modifications, but it seems to me that at heart it is the metaphysic put forth by the philosophers of the eighteenth-century Enlightenment. I do not think it is going too far to suggest that certain basic ideas, certain controlling assumptions (as the sociologists would say), lie at the heart of all our modern theories of education.

Condorcet in his "Essay on the Progress of the Mind" wrote, almost two centuries ago, that "all errors in politics and morals are based on philosophical errors. In error lies the true source of the ills that afflict the human race." Rational education, in Condorcet's view, would, by removing error (which was the equivalent of Christian sin), bring about a peaceful and orderly society.

At the end of the nineteenth century Lester Ward, the father of American sociology and a true child of the Enlightenment, wrote that the errors of the lower classes were "faith in religion, loyalty to a man, false and narrow ideas." The cure was to be education, "the salvation of the world."

The faith of the Enlightenment was elaborated into half a dozen philosophies, among them empiricism, pragmatism, logical positivism, and various forms of naturalism and scientism. Most of these philosophies were built on the assumption that individuals are by nature good, or at least neutral, and that the world can be shaped to man's desire by enlightened reason. These philosophies affected educational theory in discernible ways. On the primary and secondary level, by emphasizing the plasticity of the children, their natural goodness, and their creativity, they greatly enriched the learning experience of countless pupils. However, the progressive educators made the fundamental error of assuming that education was a "natural" process when in fact it is to the highest degree "unnatural." A corollary of this misunderstanding was their tendency to treat the child as a small adult and, under the influence of pragmatism, to put far too much emphasis on adjustment, which is a largely negative concept and a thoroughly naturalistic one. From these axioms came also the idea of education as a process of drawing knowledge out of the child, of eliciting learning, and consequently encouraging the child to speak instead of teaching him to listen. On the Enlightenment proposition that all men are equal (it was, to be sure, at first said merely that they were created equal but the "created" has been largely abandoned as a qualifier), it has been further postulated that all ideas are equal, and thus all values, those of the Hottentot with those of the Italian Renaissance.

On the college and university level, we have read a somewhat different gloss on the basic Enlightenment dogmas. Since man is basically good, and evil is simply lack of proper information, the responsibility of the university or college is to provide information. Presented with all the evidence, the student, guided by some internal monitor, will quite readily discriminate between the true and false and steer a safe course to knowledge, which is also goodness. Knowledge can be broken down into facts and the facts distributed to the students. The professor is thus a kind of intellectual retail man. In this view he is required only to have no prejudices—to push no one idea more than others. The responsibility of the teacher for research is the reverse side of his role as a disseminator of facts. He has to add to the pile, in addition to distributing it. This theory places no emphasis on the need for any real contact between student and teacher. The pretensions of the teacher are not, in general, to superior wisdom and understanding, but to more information than his students possess. The textbook and the lecture are the kingpins of this system. Information is distributed, and the student is rewarded or punished in proportion to his capacity to absorb it. The system of higher education in America, insofar as it fulfills the pattern just described, is based on an impersonal, naturalistic view of learning, and, correspondingly, of the world itself.

I do not see how we can escape the fact that modern education has its roots in a world view born in the eighteenth century and elaborated, explored, and modified—by Darwinism, pragmatism, and naturalism—in the nineteenth century. This Enlightenment view of the world is breaking up today like a giant ice floe under the batterings of contemporary history. It is no longer adequate to the needs of modern man. But the forms into which it froze continue to exist and have, moreover, considerable durability.

A change will come in both school and college education when the now obsolete metaphysic of the Enlightenment is replaced by a more human sociology that exposes the failures of the present system and shows them to be an intolerable affront to the human spirit and a vulgarization of the whole process of education.

The new metaphysical foundations of our world view are being constructed at this moment—not, of course, by professors of philosophy, who resist to the bitter end the intrusion into their carefully tended gardens of any new idea. Humanism, which has always known better, has revived its drooping spirits and come forth to do battle against materialism and its naturalistic allies. Science professes a new humility in the face of the presently impenetrable mysteries of the atom; neo-orthodoxy has stiffened the spine and deepened the faith of Protestantism. Existentialist philosophers have once more placed problems of existence, rather than of being, at the center of their thinking. Effective blows are being struck against the brutal objectification of students at the very moment in their lives when they most need to be touched, to be called by name, to be lifted out of the terrifying anonymity of the lecture hall. Nikolai Berdyaev has made wonderfully vivid the destructive nature of that spiritual solitude which comes from being nameless and objectified. "A real communion, a real triumph over solitude," he writes, "can only occur when the Ego identifies itself with the Thou, as in the case of love and friendship." If the teacher will not love the student and claim him as a friend, he cannot, unfortunately, educate him, he can only deepen his sense of alienation. We know from a dozen witnesses, among them Paul Tillich, the spiritual paralysis produced by anxiety, and it is simple enough to understand that the modern campus is a kind of hell of anxiety that can only be relieved when we speak to our students once more by name and enter into a dialogue with them. The anxiety of note taking, of anonymity, of marks, of examinations, must be transcended before education can replace instruction. This is the only educational task worth doing.

The Inhuman

| 1983 | Humanities

If patriotism is the last resort of scoundrels, it may be that the dictionary is the first recourse of an historian who has the uneasy sense that he may have bitten off more than he can chew. I have entitled my observations "The Inhuman Humanities." When I proposed that title, the subject that it suggested seemed clear enough. It still seems clear but rather more extensive than I had at first assumed.

In any event I turned to the dictionary—*Webster's Unabridged*. The dictionary definitions began with "human" and, among other definitions, offered, perhaps a bit evasively: "having or showing the qualities characteristic of people." "Humane" was defined as "having what are considered the best qualities of mankind: kind, tender, merciful, considerate. 2. civilizing, refining, humanizing; as *humane* learning." Then came "humanism," "any system or way of thought or action concerned with the interests or ideals of people. 3. the study of the humanities." Already we are in some difficulty. We are told that "humanism" is "the study of the humanities," a proposition with which we might wish to take exception. "Humanist" is then defined as "(1) a student of human nature and human affairs. (2) a student of the humanities. (3) a student of Latin and Greek culture, especially, any Renaissance scholar who was a follower of Humanism."

But we are not through. Working our way down we come to "humanistic," and "humanitarian," and then to "humanizing . . . (1) to make humane; to subdue any tendency of cruelty and to make kind, merciful, considerate, etc.; civilize, refine . . . to grow civilized; to become human or humane." Now, I think, we are at the essence of the matter. The purpose of the teaching of the "humanities" is not to convey a body of miscellaneous information in a variety of fields, it is not to drum into our heads Greek and Latin (although there are certainly worse things); it is not to make us more polished, more gentlemanly, better informed than those of our fellows not blessed with a "higher education"; it is not to bestow on us advantages of manner, of "style" as we say today, or superior income; it is, quite simply, to make us kinder, wiser, more compassionate, more "humane," in a word more human.

"In the beginning" the humanities concerned themselves with everything related to the life of man. Thus science and theology and, as soon as the words were coined, sociology and social science—the words were used virtually interchangeably—were clearly part of the domain of the humanities. *Webster's* defines the social sciences as "(a) the study of people and how they live together as families, tribes, communities, races, etc.; sociology; (b) any of several studies, as history, economics, civics, etc., dealing with the structure of society and the activities of its members." So, initially, sociology and social science were perceived as no more than extensions of the study of "the life of man."

It might not be far off the mark to suggest that "sociology" and "social science" could only begin to be outlined as fields of study in proportion as the "humanities" were more narrowly defined and as they concentrated on that new invention, "the individual." Before the appearance of the "individual" and an accompanying "individualism" and "individuality," it was difficult to deal with "human life" outside of the context of social groups, communities, and classes.

Before we move on, it might be well to emphasize one absolutely essential aspect of the humanities cum social sciences. If the intention of the study and teaching of the humanities is to make us more human, the mode in which the material that constitutes the humanities is conveyed to the student is an indivisible part of the study itself. In other words, there can be no impersonal, merely formal pedagogical procedure for transmitting that which is essential to our humanity. Large lecture halls, with hundreds of submissive students patiently transcribing impenetrable notes, are antithetical to any known civilizing or humanizing process. These may be all right for beginning chemistry, or computer science, for any study in which the simple transmission of information is the instructor's sole responsibility, but it won't do in the humanities. Here, to modify Marshall McLuhan, the method is the message. If the instructional *method* is in itself a striking denial of the instructional *content*, then clearly one is engaged in a self-defeating process.

I also think it important to shatter what may or may not be an illusion (obviously if it is not an illusion I can't shatter it). I fear that those of us who are critical of higher education sometimes talk or write as though there had been a golden age of American education. Certainly education, higher and lower, in the United States has had its ups and downs. In terms of the numbers of people to whom it has become available, its course has been steadily and in many ways spectacularly up. But by the evidence of those presumably best qualified to testify—the students or ex-students in various periods of our history—American education has, in the main, been a stultifying and depressing experience for those subjected to it. My principal witness, in this matter, will be Charles Francis Adams, Junior, writing, in his autobiography, about his experience as a Harvard undergraduate in the 1850s. The Harvard "system" seemed to Adams "radically wrong . . . . In one word: the educational trouble with Harvard in my time was the total absence of . . . direct personal influence between student and instructor. The academic, schoolmaster system prevailed . . . it was contrary to usage . . . for instructors and the instructed to hold personal relations. Our professors . . . were a set of rather eminent scholars and highly respectable men. They attended to their duties with commendable assiduity, and drudged along in a dreary humdrum sort of way in a stereotyped method of classroom instruction. But as for giving direction to, in the sense of shaping, the individual minds of the young men in their most plastic stage, so far as I know nothing of the kind was ever dreamed of. . . . This was what I needed, and all I needed – an intelligent, inspiring direction; and I never got it, nor a suggestion of it. I was left absolutely without guidance. . . . No instructor produced, or endeavored to produce, the slightest impression on me; no spark of enthusiasm was sought to be infused into me."

When Adams wrote these reflections early in the twentieth century, it was his close observation (he was a Harvard Overseer) that things were no better, indeed in some ways were worse. The Harvard system remained "the old, outgrown, pedagogic relation of the large class-recitation room. The only variation had been through [President] Eliot's effort to replace it by the yet more pernicious [German] system of premature specialization. . . . He thus made still worse what was in my time bad enough."

I hope you will believe me when I tell you that I can multiply this evidence many times over. Henry Adams (Henry wrote: "No one took Harvard seriously"), William James, Brooks Adams, John Jay Chapman, and literally dozens of others bear witness to the deplorable state of education at Harvard and elsewhere. Chapman avers that in his 1890s undergraduate days the rate of undergraduate suicides and extreme depression was so great that the Episcopal bishop of Massachusetts rallied Boston ladies to put on teas for the students to cheer them up a bit. I suppose I need hardly dwell on the fact that whatever passed for the humanities at Harvard over much of this period was thoroughly inhuman and in no substantial way fulfilled our requirement of making its students more compassionate, humane, and civilized.

To return to those studies of human life which, over half a century or so, separated themselves from the humanities and established independent academic principalities of their own, it is worth noting that one of the first Americans to use the term "social science" was that remarkable "original," John Humphrey Noyes, founder of the Perfectionist Community. Noyes believed that the careful study of social groups and Utopian experiments would disclose the "laws" of Christian socialism that should govern the lives of all of the redeemed. It was, in practical fact, this widely shared concern with reforming American society in the 1840s that stimulated interest in social science. The aim of Noyes and the early "sociologists" was to discover how to make American society more just, compassionate, and humane. To Noyes this meant applying the teachings of Jesus Christ systematically to the everyday life of the members of the Perfectionist communities. It meant, among other things, the abolition of sex distinction as regards work and play, the abolition of conventional marriage, and the complete democratization of community life.

A half century later, George Herron, the brilliant evangel of Christian socialism to the academic world, insisted that self-sacrifice was the only proper foundation for sociology. "Competitive individualism" was, Herron declared, "inconsistent with both Christianity and democracy." Like Noyes, Herron believed that "the life of man is objectively an economic life. . . . Production is communion with God. . . . "

My point is that the new fields of study found the older fields (not yet clearly defined as "humanities") too rigid and confining to accommodate their interest in the nature of the true community. Their original impulse was certainly not "scientific" in the sense in which we commonly use that word. "Science" meant to them, as it has for centuries, the careful and systematic study of phenomena whether of the human or the natural world. Social science anticipated the discovery of modes of ethical behavior that could be understood by all reasonable persons to be essential to the harmonious existence of people living together in communities, as all people did.

The spokesmen for the "new" economics and the "new" political science were similarly motivated. Richard Ely, the most influential economist of his day, was a Christian Socialist, as, apparently, was his disciple, John R. Commons. On the other hand, Lester Ward, often called the "father of American sociology," while equally idealistic and dedicated to the reform of American society, was aggressively secular.

The social sciences, born out of the struggle for social justice, rested not on scientific investigation but on a compassionate concern for the oppressed members of society. They were neither more nor less "scientific" than the older studies. They were simply, as we would say today, more "relevant" and therefore they attracted the best spirits of the day. To be sure, they were soon transformed, in their academic settings, to something quite different from what they had been in their original manifestation.

While the process that I have described was going on, a change was taking place in the American consciousness that would have a profound effect on American intellectual life and especially on that aspect of it represented by colleges and universities. *Science* was becoming the magic, talismanic word. As revealed religion in the form of Protestant Christianity had once dominated people's imagination, so science came to dominate our collective consciousness in the closing decades of the century. Everything must bear that imprimatur, even religion itself, i.e., Christian *Science*. The justified man was no longer the righteous man, he was preeminently the scientific man, the researcher, the astronomer, the chemist. Science, it was announced, had discovered a new methodology, a new way of collecting and examining evidence and of drawing conclusions or laws from it which must in time disclose the truth. The emphasis began to shift, at least in the colleges and universities, from changing the world to describing it.

In the social sciences, it was explained that the description of phenomena and the search for laws, the age of taxonomy, so to speak, was not a withdrawal from social concerns but a necessary precondition for the eventual transformation of society. The most notable aspect of the "scientific method," we were informed, was its "objectivity." It was not concerned with "value judgments," with ethical issues (except as they might appear as social "norms"). It held itself aloof from vagrant emotions and dangerous enthusiasms. Its only commitment was to the dispassionate pursuit of truth. Above all, it was devoted to the exhaustive study of minute bodies of data—specialization. Experience, it held, could only be understood piecemeal. Generalizations were suspect although, since it was impossible to suppress them, they appeared, as indeed did the despised "values," in various ingenious disguises.

While there was a deceptive plausibility, perhaps inevitability, about the course that the social sciences took—that is to say their growing insistence that they were "scientific" and "objective" and their imperial ambitions (they gobbled up psychology and anthropology and tried, with limited success, to seduce history)—there seemed to be far less logic in the efforts of those fields that remained outside of the enchanted circle to emulate science. These fields included literature, which expanded to take in a number of "new" or only distantly related fields such as languages, philosophy, history, and, more recently, the arts—music, the history of art, drama, even the crafts.

The movement to "scientize" higher education did not triumph without a struggle. The key figure in that struggle was William James, although there are a number of less well-known heroes. Single-handedly, James infused a substantial segment of Harvard with his enthusiasm for learning, for the things which "enlighten and ennoble." Starting off as a young instructor in anatomy, he moved in time to psychology, laying the foundation for that study, and then on to philosophy. With the somewhat bewildered support of Eliot he was able to attract a number of stars—Josiah Royce, sometimes Charles Sanders Peirce, George Santayana, and, finally, that Germanic oddity, Hugo Münsterberg.

James was like the prince in a fairy tale who awakened an old slumbering crone, Harvard College, with a kiss and for a decade or two transformed her into a beautiful young muse. Enthusiasm and love are an irresistible combination. James drew the best students to him like a magnet. He urged them to acquire "mental perspective." "Is there," he asked them, "space and air in your mind, or must your companions gasp for breath whenever they talk with you?" What students must catch from their teachers, he wrote, was "the living, philosophic attitude of mind, the independent personal look at all the data of life. . . ."

The brilliant black student, W. E. B. Du Bois, the Hapgood brothers, Norman and Hutchins from the Midwest, John Jay Chapman, Walter Lippmann, and literally dozens of others drew life and inspiration from him. One man who embodied humane learning made Harvard a fountainhead of intellectual energy. "Every year I hear more about you," Chapman wrote his former teacher, "and I know you have put life into your whole science all over the country. I see the younger generation—run across them in one way or another—and trace back their vitality to you."

James refused to be overawed by the scientists. "Their interests are most incomplete and their professional conceit and bigotry immense. I know no narrower sect or club," he wrote. But even James could not turn the heavy-running tide of scientism. Harvard calcified around him. Younger academics criticized his "personal" style. He was not objective enough. He put too much of himself into his teaching and writing. Chapman noted that there was a definite bias at Harvard against young teachers who showed what was considered excessive enthusiasm for their subjects (or their students). They were not kept; more objective types were preferred. By the turn of the century the game was pretty well lost. James was glad to retire. Harvard had come to place more faith in bibliographies, he noted wryly, than in trying to touch fire in young minds.

Interestingly, the struggle between what I suppose we should properly call the "new humanistic impulse" as represented by individuals like William James, Charles Sanders Peirce, Josiah Royce, and Woodrow Wilson and the new specialized scholarship was represented geographically and architecturally at Princeton. There Wilson, the new president of the university, was determined that the grand Gothic-style graduate school designed by Ralph Adams Cram be located in close proximity to the undergraduate college to symbolize and facilitate intellectual interaction between young students and more mature scholars. Wilson was defeated. Cram's Gothic towers rose a considerable distance from the college. There graduate students, aping admired British customs, wore their academic robes to "high table." The crowning irony was that the Oxbridge model, which they tried to emulate in dress and architecture, represented just that interplay between seasoned scholar-teachers and students that Wilson was determined to introduce into Princeton. Superficial formalities won but the spirit was lost. Behind facades that attempted to evoke the ideal of a classical education for English gentlemen, German scholarship of the most morally debilitating kind flourished. Like James, Wilson deplored the divorce of higher learning from an audience of intelligent laymen.

By the outbreak of World War I, the modern university was clearly defined. It was committed wholeheartedly, or perhaps it may be fairer to say that it was committed half-heartedly, since pockets of resistance remained in state universities and small private so-called liberal arts colleges to specialized "objective" research whose results were embalmed in monographs. The state universities, in counterdistinction to the private colleges, persisted in using "research" to collect the facts that must underlie any comprehensive reform of the capitalist system.

The reasons for the growing rigidity, excessive specialization, and coldness of spirit that increasingly characterized higher education are not easy to unravel. The socialists, of whom there were a considerable number, blamed capitalism. Capitalists would only shower their benefactions on institutions of higher learning if outspoken professors with radical opinions were fired or bullied into silence. John D. Rockefeller withheld several millions until William Rainey Harper, president of the University of Chicago, had silenced a pesky professor, Edward Bemis, who supported the municipal ownership of public utilities. As detached an observer of the American scene as Brooks Adams was convinced there was a clear cause-and-effect relationship between the withdrawal of professors from politically sensitive issues to specialized and politically innocuous scholarship and pressures from wealthy benefactors. Adams wrote in 1912, "In the United States capital has long owned the leading universities by right of purchase, as it has owned the highways [railroads], the currency, and the press, and capital has used the universities, in a general way, to develop capitalistic ideas." But this was not Adams's most serious charge. "Apparently," he wrote, "modern society, if it is to cohere, must have a high order of generalizing mind—a mind which can grasp a multitude of complex relations. . . . Capital has preferred the specialized mind and that not of the highest quality, since it has found it profitable to set quantity before quality to the limit the market will endure. Capitalists have never insisted upon raising an educational standard save in science and mechanics, and the relative overstimulation of the scientific mind has now become an actual menace to order. . . . "

One result of the assault by capitalists on professors who expressed opinions unpopular with trustees was the emergence of the idea of tenure. Once a professor had established his competence as a scholar and teacher, the notion went, he could not be fired without serious cause such as moral turpitude. Although the principle of tenure was often more honored in the breach than the observance, it did indicate a commendable solicitude for academic free speech. The problem was that it was accompanied by a growing acceptance of the notion that the true scholar was objective and impartial. At least as far as his teaching was concerned, he should remain aloof from controversial social and political issues. Since he might be assumed to have strong feelings on such matters, it was important that he refrain from allowing his own emotions to influence his teaching and thereby the presumably impressionable young men and women who attended his lectures. But it proved impossible to divorce the academic world from politics. During World

War I, professors who opposed the entry of the United States into the conflict or espoused pacifism were usually summarily fired, tenure or no tenure. The story was repeated in the era of the "Red scare" that followed the war and again with the rise of the Cold War between Russia and the United States after World War II. Inspired by the House Un-American Activities Committee's investigations into subversion, universities from Harvard to California sacked professors who confessed to communist inclinations or merely refused, on the grounds of conscience, to sign an oath affirming their loyalty to the United States. The justification for such firings was that scholars were supposed to be impartial and objective. If you were of Marxist persuasion, you had given your allegiance to a particular political and philosophical system (and an "alien" one at that) and thus could not properly discharge your academic responsibility to be wholly objective. That serious and reasonably intelligent men could have subscribed to such a transparently flimsy proposition is a wonder until we recall the power of received opinion whereby patently false propositions once accepted, for whatever reasons, quickly turn into impregnable dogmas or, more modestly, unexamined assumptions.

It is my perception that the illusion of objectivity, of scientific detachment as applied to the humanities cum social sciences, has lost its credibility. Marxists now proclaim their "scientific" dogmas quite freely on campuses all around the country and if their tenets are, in the main, depressingly sterile, the fact that they are free to teach them is certainly a sign of progress. But it cannot be too strongly emphasized that we continue to behave *as though* the old dogmas still retained their efficacy. All our academic arrangements are based on those no-longer-believed-in assumptions. To face the facts would mean a complete restructuring of higher education and that, obviously, we are not disposed to do.

While it would probably be unfair to say that the academic world remained dormant through the period from, say, 1914 to 1945, it is certainly true that the boom and depression years meant, of necessity, that relatively little attention was given to educational philosophy. Yet the growth of higher education was steady. Between 1880 and 1920, a span of forty years, the number of B.A.'s awarded increased from 13,000 to

61,000. From 1922 to 1940, the number swelled from 61,000 to 186,000, a more than three-fold increase in a period of eighteen years. In 1880, the ratio of B.A.'s was nineteen for every 1,000 persons of college age. In 1940, that figure had risen to eighty-one. At the same time, the percentage of high school graduates going to college dropped from fifty-nine per hundred in 1885 to eighteen per hundred in 1940. Those figures reflect, of course, the relatively low number of students completing high school in the earlier year.

Between 1922 and 1940, the number of doctorates awarded rose from 780 to 3,276. Of the 3,276 awarded in 1940, 433 were in the so-called social sciences—125 in economics and 129 in psychology. The so-called humanities had a total of 628, of which 167 were in history, 354 in language and literature, and 107 in "other," primarily the "arts." If, following the Smith logic, we combine the humanities and the social sciences on the grounds that the original division was, in any event, meaningless and misleading, we get a total of 1,061 in what we might call "human studies," or roughly one-third of the total number of doctorates awarded.

Thirty years later, in 1970, the picture had changed in instructive ways. Of the 29,479 doctoral degrees granted in that year, 5,563 were in the so-called social sciences (1,888 were in psychology, economics was second with 853, political science lagged in fourth place with 635). In the so-called humanities, literature and language led; the arts, the despised "other" of our earlier figures, had taken over second place with 1,138, and history held fairly firm at 1,092. But in terms of relative position as measured at least by Ph.D's, the humanities lost ground to the social sciences—4,060 to 5,563. The most spectacular growth had been in psychology and in the arts, which, in the same period, rose from 107 to 1,138. Statistics are, admittedly, slippery items but they are useful in pointing out trends and even more in correcting misapprehensions. The spectacular rise in psychology and the arts in relation to the older disciplines certainly conveys a message. We may, of course, differ in the interpretation of that message. For me, it reinforces one of my basic propositions—to wit, that the "humanities" have failed in their traditional mission of making their students "more humane, more kind, merciful, considerate, etc.," more conscious of what it means, in the last analysis, to be human. The consequence is that students have gravitated to those studies that at least seemed to promise better things—psychology and art (I certainly am under no illusion that the greater part of academic psychology in fact fulfills that promise. But it at least talks about people and their problems). Now that the arts are having a boom, the humanities seem more charitably disposed toward them after giving them the cold shoulder for years. But this, of course, all begs the point. It is merely symptomatic. Psychology plus the arts cannot assume the classic mission of the kingpins of the humanities— literature and history.

The education "explosion" that followed World War II exaggerated all the flaws and deficiencies that had been evident by the early decades of the century. In the aggregate it constituted a kind of academic "gold rush." Departments used graduate study to build academic empires. Publication, which had been encouraged in a few ambitious institutions, was now required everywhere. Academic ratings, prestige, grants—everything depended on it. Let a merciful silence shroud the consequences. I have not found a knowledgeable "informant" able to explain to me how "learning" or "humanity" or "humanism" was served thereby.

While the results of specialized scholarship are, on the whole, depressingly meager, it might be argued that the principal burden of this strange infatuation has fallen upon the students and the general public. The *General Catalogue* of the University of California at Santa Cruz for the year 1981–1982 listed fifteen faculty members in history (Santa Cruz is a comparatively small campus with only some 6,000 students). These fifteen faculty members offered, or had listed in the catalogue, seventy-eight courses. These ranged from general lower-division courses such as "The Classical World," "The History of American Slavery," and "Urban Ethnic Groups" to the familiar little segments of history common to virtually all college catalogues—"Topics in Chicano History," "Socialism and Communism in the Nineteenth and Twentieth Centuries," "World War I," "Native People in Latin America," "Modern Life in Japan," "The World and the Imperialist West," and "Peasants and Artisans in French History." It is hard to object to any of these courses in and of themselves. They are undoubtedly taught

with varying degrees of success by well-informed, competent instructors. But one looks in vain for a principle of coherence in the history
curriculum, for some common notion of history, or the study thereof.
The only determinants are apparently the research interests of particular professors each of whom clearly has as much right to teach what he
wishes as his colleagues. I have done it myself. Several years back I
taught a course entitled "Anxiety and Despair; Guilt, Suffering, and
Sin in American History." There is one common theme by default, so
to speak. Except in a course in "historical methodology," no history
major is required to read—or perhaps more accurately, all are discouraged from reading—any of the great historians of the past (the methodology course points out how superior present-day methodology is to
the hopelessly out-dated methodologies of less enlightened eras). It is
not necessary to read those old, discredited historians, the students are
assured, because modern research has proved them "wrong." (I wonder!) (Incidentally, Woodrow Wilson, deploring the direction of academic history early in the present century, suggested that its practitioners be called "historical investigators" on the grounds that the word
"historian" should be reserved for those who wrote history in the tradition of Thucydides, Gibbon, Macaulay, and, in America, Parkman,
Prescott, and Motley.)

Of course, the academic historians do not admit that they are engaged in a form of modern scholasticism where the means have become
far more important than the ends. They assure puzzled inquirers who
ask to what end their labors are directed that they are in relentless pursuit, aided increasingly by computers, of the truth about man's past. But
when will that be revealed? When will the monographs all be added up
or fitted together (and by what superior intelligence?) and the general
public let in on the now-so-carefully-guarded truth? Sometime in the
rapidly receding future when all the knots have been unraveled, the
gaps filled in, the faulty or incomplete studies done or redone. Mean-
time, we wither on the vine for lack of history, for lack of humane letters, for lack of information about man's common life, social man, cultural man, political man, economic man, just plain man in all his
astonishing multiformity.

So much for history. In the most recent issue of the *Harvard Maga-*

zine, W. Jackson Bate, a senior professor in the Department of English at that university, writes, "The humanities are not merely entering, they are plunging into their worst state of crisis since the modern university was formed ... they seem bent on a self-destructive course through a combination of anger, fear, and purblind defensiveness." Bate then goes on to spell out the nature and consequences of this decline as they relate specifically to departments of English. His analysis reinforces my own, especially with respect to the perniciousness of the publish-or-perish syndrome.

Perhaps the most striking, if indirect, consequence of the retreat of the academic world from consideration of the classic question, in the words of the late Nelson Algren—"What is Man?"—into its own self-absorption, is the replacement of what I call the "preacherly tradition" by the "priestly tradition." At the heart of the Protestant Passion was the conviction that individuals could know God best through the exercise of their own faculties, through "reason" in the large and ancient meaning of that word, through mind illuminated by faith. In that effort one found aid and guidance from leaders specially trained in interpreting God's word, the elected preachers and ministers who led the elect. From John Winthrop and Roger Williams to Ralph Waldo Emerson, Horace Bushnell, Wendell Phillips, Washington Gladden, William James, Charles Sanders Peirce, and thousands of other less well-known preacher-intellectuals, religious and lay, the generality of Americans received through sermons, lectures, journals, magazines, and the public press illumination in all matters relating to manners and morals, to ethical imperatives, to social issues and public policy. With the emergence of the university as the center of intellectual activity in our society, the preacherly function of the intellectual was replaced by the priestly function. The canons of the profession held that scholarship was an essentially esoteric undertaking based on highly specialized learning and, increasingly, on an intricate "methodology" and a technical language known only to the initiate.

Professor-scholars' first loyalty was not to the institutions that employed them (they changed these as casually as they changed clothes) or to the undergraduate students who sat passively in their classes but to their *disciplines* and, above all, to their *fields,* those areas of specialization within their disciplines to which they devoted their academic lives. It was what we might call a "trickle-down" theory of education. If scholars pursued their researches single-mindedly, some of the more comprehensible elements presumably would appear in the specialized courses that they taught undergraduates.

I believe that many of our psychic disorders, failures of will or morale, the slackness of spirit that seems to characterize our times is the consequence of having most of those who should be our natural intellectual and moral leaders confined to the cloistered halls of the academy. It is bad for them and bad for us. They pursue their minute investigations in airless and fluorescent corridors, diminished in mind and soul, while we pine for those inspiring words that would lift our hearts and point a path for our footsteps. How strange and sad that we should come at the end of the twentieth century to this bitter impasse, our tongues confused, our councils divided!

Many professors blame the erosion of the humanities on the crassness of the modern student, more interested in making money than in pursuing humane learning. We blame it on the stinginess of the state legislatures or reactionary policies in Washington, on the glamour that envelops the physical sciences, or on the trendiness of environmental studies. In short, on everything except ourselves.

I think we can accept it as a fact that all human beings have, in the words of a colleague of mine, at least "a small insect-like emotional life," and that emotional life yearns desperately to be fed, to be enlarged and enhanced, to be encouraged to believe that there is, after all, something noble about human existence, that it has a meaning even if the meaning is no more than the poignant and tireless effort generation after generation to understand its meaning. We wish, in at least a part of us, to be wiser, kinder, more considerate, more compassionate. We know instinctively that these aspirations must be nurtured, as a mother gives nurture to her child, and, further, that our hopes look beyond our narrow, selfish interests to the needs and concerns of others and beyond our own lives to the lives of future generations. We know too that our most basic task may be the transmission of the best values we have inherited so that man may endure.

If we wish to use the word "humanities" in the fullest and best meaning of the word and all its associated words and connotations without blushing, then we had best look into our hearts and ask if we have been faithful witnesses to and custodians of a great tradition. Inextricably intertwined with that question, part and parcel of it, the beginning of any conceivable reformation, is the question of our responsibility to our students. If we do not love and care for them, if we do not place them in the center of our thinking and doing, if we persist in thinking that they are merely incidental to or distracting from our serious scholarly concerns, then there is, quite literally, no hope for higher education. Only a few of us can be scholars in the deepest and best meaning of that word (and I certainly do not count myself in that number); not all of us can be "great teachers" and win awards as the teacher of the year with a plaque and cash bonus. But all of us who profess to be concerned with the humanities can learn in association with our students—with and through them—how to be more human. That is the only way I can perceive to rescue the humanities from a fate truly worse than death, from frozen rectitude and self-preoccupation.

Tenure:

Pushing Back the Frontiers of Knowledge

I was interested in Tom Kennedy's article on "Publish or Perish" (*City on the Hill Press*, April 16). Like an old cavalry charger at the sound of a bugle, a reference to P or P brings out my martial ardor. I left the University in 1973 not only because of a particular injustice, but also because of my belief that the intellectual and moral falsity of P or P was poisoning the atmosphere of scholarship and teaching.

In my view the whole P or P proposition rests on certain unexamined and, I believe, completely untenable assumptions.

The first of these is what might be called *the fallacy of misplaced scientism*. From this fallacy flow many of the ills of the modern university.

The fallacy of misplaced scientism goes something like this: human society is "progressive," that is to say, in all fields of human endeavor we are accumulating more and more information capable of being transformed into knowledge, which in turn brings us, inevitably, closer and closer to the truth. In the academic world this progressive movement is carried forward by what is called research. Research is, essentially, the intensive and, one hopes, exhaustive examination of limited amounts of data, of carefully circumscribed "problems," and so on. Each of these pieces of research, each of these monographs, is presumed to be like a little experiment performed in a laboratory. Once performed, once a monograph is written on, say, to take a famous example, the *Wisconsin Dairy Industry from 1880 to 1890*, it need never be done again; it becomes an increment in a far larger study of the Wisconsin dairy industry from the arrival of the first cow and the first farmer down to the present day, and the full, grand, and complete story of the Wisconsin dairy industry becomes, in turn, part of the whole of American, and indeed, world history. In the phrase so beloved of academic administrators, "it pushes forward the frontiers of knowledge" although just where it pushes them is not at all clear.

Now if we were to grant the premise of the P or P people—that every university, or, perhaps better, every "great" university like the University of California, is dedicated to "pushing back the frontiers of knowledge," we might be able to justify sacking those who didn't seem to be doing their share of pushing. But the fact is that in those studies concerned with the human as opposed to the physical world, there is, regrettably, no evidence that knowledge (or understanding) is progressive or cumulative. There is, for example, no evidence that the vast accumulation of monographs on Shakespeare have added substantially to the pleasure and instruction with which the ordinary citizen reads Shakespeare. Nor is there any evidence that more than a century of highly specialized study of American history has in any systematic, "scientific" way increased our understanding of that strange drama. American historians have been writing these pushing-back-the-frontiers-of-knowledge monographs for the past eighty or one hundred years—often for no better reason than to avoid perishing—and we now have far more than the most industrious scholar can read in a lifetime. They clutter the shelves of university libraries and clog the warehouses of university presses. Published in minute editions, they are soon remaindered at a fraction of their excessive cost. Who reads them and what frontiers are they pushing back? All we can say with certainty is that the time spent writing them is taken from the teaching of students, and the writing of them is in large part coerced, a condition of continued employment. Whatever else they are or whatever else they may do, they seldom make life pleasanter or more understandable or even more endurable. I certainly have nothing against monographs per se. I ask only that they be the lively result of some scholar's passionate involvement in a subject that may seem trivial until he or she convinces us otherwise.

Let me make myself clear. It is irrefutable that we know more, or at least have more knowledge available to us, than ever before. But that we are wiser or better for it is by no means evident. Nor in the areas of human or social studies is there any reason to believe that we are "progressing" by virtue of "research." Research is, of course, one of the great totems of our time. It assuredly covers a multitude of sins (most of them against students) but it has such a marvelously reassuring resonance about it that I suspect we will never give it up. To the question, "What are you doing these days?" the answer "Research" has about it an air of sanctity that hardly another word in our lexicon possesses. To be "in research" is the equivalent, in an earlier age, of being in a state of grace.

A recently issued chancellorian "bull" attempting for the Nth time to explain and justify the university's policy in awarding tenure declares, "We do *not* . . . advocate reward for those who do not perform their fundamental scholarly function of research with outstanding skill." Several comments may be in order. Since the Chancellor is a scientist there is, inevitably I suspect, a certain discontinuity when he undertakes to speak to workers in the nonsciences. In the "humanistic disciplines" (not a phrase I much like), research consists, in large part, of reading other people's books and writing notes thereon on little cards, and I am not sure that the notion of "skill" is relevant to such an activity. What, for example, should be the "research" required of an assistant professor of American history? It would seem to me to be to read as widely as possible and think as tenaciously as possible (clearly giving preference to the latter function) about American history. But is this research in the sense in which the Chancellor uses the word? I suspect not. Something that "pushes back the frontiers of knowledge," something that, *above all, results in a published monograph.* So the Chancellor is not talking about *research*; he is talking about *publication.* But why insist on publication; why not simply try to agree on some sensible definition of research or, more modestly, "intelligent scholarly activity"? The ostensible reason for publication is so that one's colleagues can be informed of the consequences of one's research. But why do they need to know? So that they can immediately incorporate this new insight or discovery into their own teaching and writing. Here is demonstrated the *fallacy of misplaced scientism.* The Chancellor's proposition may be unassailable in the area of genetics or atomic physics, but it has very little relevance in such fields as history, philosophy, and literature, where even the word "research" is misleading and, to a degree at least, irrelevant. "Skill in research" means nothing in the field of history. It is here entirely a matter of what historians do with their research. They can pile it as high as Everest, and if they do not turn it, at least in some modest measure, into art, they had better leave it in the pile.

The argument over P and P can never be resolved as long as we give credence to the notion that the eminence of an institution of higher learning (or its closeness to the heart of the Almighty) is to be measured by the monolith of monographs extracted from overworked scholars. Rather we should be trying to prevail on our colleagues not to add one single increment to that monstrously swollen pile unless they simply can't help it. To write a book is, in any proper existential sense, an absurd undertaking, vain, risky, egotistical, problematic in the extreme.

What, then, should be going on in universities if not the slavish writing of monographs in order to secure tenure? Quite evidently, it should be the complicated, arduous, but highly rewarding process of education.

Human Time
1957 and the
College Student

The tension in the large room is almost palpable. The air is tainted with the odor of sweat. The faces of the men and women are drawn and taut. Their bodies are twisted in postures of agonized thought, of supplication, of despair. The scene is not that of a torture chamber but of a roomful of students taking a final examination.

Surely a professor's most disheartening experience is to patrol the classroom during the final examination for his course. If he has tried to make the course a vital one, if he has tried to catch the students up in an adventure of learning that has contained some joy and play as well as high seriousness, he cannot but feel downhearted as he watches their strained faces, observes their exhaustion and anxiety. This is certainly a dismal end to an at least theoretically enlivening experience. Only convention can make it tolerable to the professor and his students. We are bound to ask ourselves, it seems to me, how well the aims of a particular course or of education in general are served by this ordeal. Its avowed purpose is to make sure that the student has accomplished something measurable in mastering a certain body of material, that he has increased his efficiency or his knowledge. We assure ourselves that the final examination accomplishes this, but we have ample testimony that it does not. I suspect that most of us have little conviction that six years or six months after the completion of this or that course, its graduates could pass even a vastly simplified examination on its content. What we might call the "retention quotient" is, in most courses, very low indeed. There is much to suggest that because the final examination presents both a frightening hurdle and an obvious terminus, it actually inhibits retention of the course content. Students at least believe so and often speak cynically of final examinations as a kind of intellectual purge by which the mind is evacuated of all the material that has been stored in it during the course.

It should be obvious that the typical examination is not the proper means to ensure the student's carrying away from the work of a semester an important residue of information or knowledge. It does give us, however, a conviction that we are discriminating, that we are forcing the student to comply with certain standards, that we have transferred, even if on a temporary basis, certain information to our passive auditors. What is perhaps most important of all, we have provided a means by which the student's advance toward his ultimate goal—a degree—can be measured. Using it we are able to assign a "mark" which presumably measures the student's accomplishment. And this mark is an integral part of our educational process.

While the final examination is only the concluding trial of the average course, we might take it as a symbol of much that is wrong with our instructional methods on the college level. The fact is that our colleges are, to a considerable degree, neither subject-oriented nor student-oriented but mark-oriented. They are set up, on the undergraduate level, to facilitate the awarding and the recording of marks. Individual courses of instruction are almost invariably organized with an eye on marking procedures. In large courses where the instructor is assisted by graduate students who read and grade the papers, it is especially important to devise examinations that require essentially factual answers. These answers may be in the form of multiple choices, in which case they are often graded by a machine, or they may be in the form of an essay. The essay-type question is an improvement over the true-false or multiple-choice examination since it requires that the student be more or less literate. But in practice this type of examination must still place its emphasis on the factual in order to make possible a uniform system of grading by one or more "readers."

However much, in courses of this kind, the professor may affirm his desire to have the students "think for themselves," the students cannot in fact do so. Ideal answers in these mass-administered and mass-graded tests have to be devised and marks awarded on the basis of the number of essential points included in each answer. Such courses, moreover, are usually taught in conjunction with a textbook, and here the student's impulse, not unnaturally, is to memorize the text at the expense of a thoughtful, critical review of the lecture material. The large lecture courses which use a textbook and in which the grading is done by "readers" or "assistants" are self-defeating. The complex, unfamiliar, and elusive ideas given in lectures cannot compete successfully, in most instances, with the neatly assembled data in the textbook. The student is further discouraged in any speculation by the consciousness that he may have missed or misunderstood the precise point the lecturer was trying to make and may thus render it up in mutilated or unrecognizable form.

Let us assume that the student accepts the invitation to "think for himself." In most cases his thoughts will be confused and banal, a mishmash of rather unformed ideas that he has picked up in high-school civics courses, at home, from random reading, from movies and television. They will not be worth much in terms of a mark. How is the professor, or his surrogate, the reader, to react? Does he give the student an A for effort, thus encouraging him in the idea that he is a thinker of considerable power and originality? Or does he admonish him gently and give him a C, thus confirming the student's suspicions that the professor never meant what he said anyway?

Again the mark is the culprit. The fact is that the mark should be used only as an incentive, as a corrective, as a stimulus. A first-rate student often needs to be most severely marked for sloppy thinking, for intellectual short cuts, for the facile use of academic clichés. As a Cambridge tutor expressed it to me, "The teacher should be free, if the character of the student suggests it is the best course, to tear up his paper before him, denounce his work as careless and inaccurate, berate him soundly, and send him off to do the work of which he is capable." Perhaps the student who suffers most under our marking system is the outstanding individual who, in any comparison with his fellows, must be given an A and thus cannot be treated with the rigor that would eventually make the most of his superior capacities.

Since all marks are carefully recorded, added up, weighed and assessed, and stand unalterable upon the student's record, they cannot be used with any real freedom or flexibility. Most of us are reluctant to give a mark that will perhaps count against a scholarship, a job, or a cherished academic plum.

I suspect that largely as a result of the grading system a majority of the students regard the professor as, in a sense, the enemy. That is to say, the professor represents an unknown quantity that has the potentiality of damaging the student. As professor he is in a position of almost unlimited power. To counter this the student has a kind of cunning which he has acquired as a by-product of the educational process. He is conditioned to play the game according to the rules. He knows that if, like the psychologist's pigeon, he pecks the right button, he will get a kernel of corn. He has, therefore, very little to gain and much to lose by taking liberties with the system. The prevailing educational conventions combine to make him cagey. He knows that his teachers are at least partly human and that however remote most of them may seem from his real life and interests, they have their crotchets, their small vanities, and their prejudices. At the beginning of a class the student is alert to penetrate these and to discern in what way they can be made to work to his advantage. He knows that despite a pretense of professional objectivity, the instructor has a fairly well-developed set of biases, and the student welcomes evidences of these because they are guideposts to him. Correspondingly, the absence of discernible prejudices is unsettling for the student—it means another anxiety-producing unknown element in the equation that should yield up the desired mark.

The only way that the professor can overcome the student's habit of calculation, which is generally fatal to the learning process, is by lessening some of his apprehensions. The student's attitude is indeed ambivalent, and this is the professor's opportunity. In addition to their feelings of anxiety and hostility, many students genuinely wish to be touched and affected by the professor. The student has had, in his learning experience, a few teachers who have done this and he knows that, while it is unlikely, it can happen. But the professor, in his efforts to create this kind of *rapport*, is at a disadvantage. He is inviting a confidence that he cannot honor. The student may in fact be drawn from his shell and inspired to venture some independent judgment, but the assessment of this hesitant enterprise will not be made by the man who has solicited it but, in many instances, by a third party, the reader.

Even if it were possible to set up a grading procedure by which efforts at original and independent thinking would be encouraged and rewarded, there would still be little incentive for the bright student to make the effort. Being examination-oriented and acutely mark-conscious, he knows that there is always an element of chance in examinations and he has a strong impulse to keep this to a minimum.

He realizes that it is often not so much what he knows as how much mileage he can get out of the information that he has committed to memory. The means of testing now used in most colleges and universities often fall short of measuring the excellence or the capacity of the student. For the most part they record his ability to memorize and record a certain rather narrow range of information, and here technique is of great importance. If, by the painstaking accumulation of facts and approved theories and their careful regurgitation, the student can get the desired mark, he is borrowing trouble to attempt something more ambitious.

The teacher is, of course, as much the victim of our testing conventions as the student is. Examinations play an important part in his conception of himself as teacher and scholar. Not infrequently he comes to view them as weapons in a contest between himself and his students. Unexpected and unorthodox questions affirm his "toughness" and give a comforting spread in marks. Even in the most straightforward examination, some conscientious students will have failed to prepare certain questions adequately since all the significant material in a given course can seldom be mastered with complete thoroughness and an element of chance inevitably enters in. Difficult and obscure questions will scatter the field even further, reducing the number of A's and B's and giving the professor the reassuring feeling that he is a stern marker who is upholding "standards."

It might be said that the whole matter of "distribution" and grading on the "curve" is one of the most patent fallacies in the marking system. It seems to be based on the assumption that the student population in any particular course should be spread out with a certain percentage of

A's, B's, C's, and so on, but this assumption, which is treated by many professors with the sanctity of a kind of natural law of education, will not bear close scrutiny. It is certainly conceivable that rigorous and demanding courses can be given to large numbers of students in which no "proper" distribution occurs. When this happens, however, the professor involved often feels under compulsion to revamp his testing techniques to produce a result more in accord with accepted practice lest his colleagues suspect that he is "soft" or perhaps trying to win students by relaxed standards—a kind of academic scab who is willing to accept less than the prevailing scale.

What I have to say about the inadequacies of the marking system applies most directly to freshman and sophomore "survey" courses taken by large numbers of students who, it is hoped, will thereby get a nodding acquaintance with, say, Western Civilization, or Art in World History, or Patterns of Social Development. My strictures apply with somewhat less force to the more advanced courses, but even here, especially in the larger institutions, readers are in evidence, and the more onerous features of the grading system are only slightly ameliorated.

In the first place, by the time they are upperclassmen, the majority of students are thoroughly conditioned to the corruption of marks, and it is correspondingly difficult to break through to the individual, to lure him into any free and uninhibited expression of feeling or opinion. As an advanced student he has found his level—A, B, or C. He knows what kind of effort is required to maintain it in the average course, provided again that the student-intelligence service is functioning effectively.

The student accepts the system because it can be figured out, anticipated, and made, in general, to yield the desired token. The professor often values it for its very impersonality, or "objectivity." Every student, if he is known, presents the teacher with a unique problem. Is the middle-aged schoolteacher from Louisiana, seeking a salary increase by the accumulation of additional course credits, to be judged by the same standards as the brilliant and precocious high school student, or the man with two children who works twenty or thirty hours a week, or the boy who works on a night shift in a railroad yard to help put a younger brother through school, or the housewife who wishes to secure a pri-

mary-school teaching credential? Perhaps it can be argued that these
are extreme cases, but our existing canons of grading dictate that we
treat all individuals the same way.

Now this is not quite as bad if we are giving an essentially professional
education to a homogeneous student body with a common cultural
background, but if this is no longer our basic task, the only alternative
is to attempt to assess each student individually. Of course, such a suggestion alarms the bureaucrats since it involves difficult and dangerous
decisions on the part of the professor and smacks of the "progressive"
ideas that most of us view with suspicion when we observe them in operation on the secondary-school level. But it might be answered that
the failure of the secondary schools is not so much caused by trying to
meet the needs of the individual student as it is by watering down and
destroying the content of the traditional curriculum in the name of "adjustment" or of "practical" education. If the liberal arts curriculum is
maintained and strengthened as the heart of higher education, the effort to adopt a more flexible and more personal approach to the student
can only be salutary in its effects. Both the mediocre and the outstanding student will profit from such a change in emphasis, and standards,
instead of being lowered, will be raised, since the student who is in a
one-to-one relationship to his teacher will more often have his best efforts evoked.

The answer to such proposals will, of course, be that the present ratio
of professors to students is not great enough to permit attention to the
needs and capacities of individual students. I believe that there is much
that can be done within the existing framework of most college and university curriculums without submerging the professor, but it is probably
true that some institutional reforms are needed to reduce the rigidity of
the present system. In any event, a necessary first step toward breaking
the tyranny of the marking and examination system is the frank admission that these are at best necessary evils that have about them no savor
of salvation, but rather, by their own interior logic, work toward the
increasing formalization of higher education. Perhaps an uprising
against the existing practices should begin with the destruction of the
I.B.M. machines and the dispersion of those who tend them, followed
by the rout of the academic bureaucrats.

Such a revolt would open the way for the establishment of more human and more flexible procedures. One hesitates to say what these procedures should be. Perhaps it is enough, at this stage, to insist that time spans must be created for the student that will relieve him of the continual anxiety of recurrent tests and examinations. The fragmentation of the student's learning experience seriously inhibits his intellectual growth and his personal development. Information can be dispensed on a unit basis, but formation and re-formation require unbroken increments of time. In our present curriculum all marks, all assignments, all chapters are of equal significance because, as weighed by a mark, all weigh the same. The trivial takes equal rank with the important and the student's power of discrimination is soon lost.

A renewed dialogue, the creation of generous time spans, the bold and unabashed reenactment of the historic drama of the self confronting the cosmos, these are the directions American higher education must take if it is not to degenerate into a fact mill or a colossal trade school.

Students Don't "Study" History—
They Are History

1977

As a historian who has taught elementary, secondary, college, and graduate students, I have misgivings about whether history should be taught in school at all.

It is my belief that a child experiences the world with a particular kind of immediacy. An event a month in the future seems an interminable time away. Time past is bound by the child's memory. Historical time is infinitely remote and unreal. Many adults live in this "childish" time most of their lives. Others gain historical perspective or "consciousness" that enables them to get a sense of their relationship to past experience and history. One familiar example is the indifference most of us felt as children to the "history" of our parents and grandparents. Later, when they were dead, we longed to be able to quiz them about the history that they had experienced. Obviously, our interest in history in general grows as we acquire more and more personal history and reflect upon its meaning. We are faced then, as teachers of history, with the problem of having to teach too soon.

In conformity to state law, a certain amount of history is taught in primary and secondary schools under the rubric of social studies, especially the history of the pupil's own state and nation. Granting that state legislators and school boards are going to insist on a minimum amount of history being taught at the primary and secondary school levels, even if students haven't become aware of themselves as historical beings, the question is: how is history to be taught?

I suppose for many students the most dismal part of historical study is committing to memory certain selected historical facts: the dates of battles, the names of presidents and generals, and on and on. It is not necessary to describe here how the study of history came to be confused with the rote learning of names and dates. One can pass by that chapter in intellectual and academic history and simply say, in agreement with the historian Egon Friedell, that there is nothing more contemptible than a fact. The living spirit of history, while certainly not indifferent to facts, rises splendidly above them. The Crystal Palace, for example, was built in 1851, sponsored by the Royal Society of the Arts and designed by Sir Joseph Paxton. It was considered one of the wonders of the world, a structure of prefabricated iron units, glass, and wood, built in London to house the Exhibition of 1851. Facts. But the potency of the structure must be experienced in quite another way. It must be imaginatively entered into (or actually entered into when possible). Facts must be transmuted into experience.

HISTORY AS EXPERIENCE

The poor benighted history student learns facts in the same spirit that chemistry students learn the elements in various compounds. It has always been a minor embarrassment to me that I have a wretched memory and can never recall any "facts" about American history. Acquaintances often turn to me for the commonplace items of American history: "Wasn't it Cleveland who ran for President in 1892?" Or: "When was the Missouri Compromise passed?" Or: "What were the terms of the Gadsden Purchase?" My reply is almost invariably an unhappy mumble: "I'm afraid I don't remember." That the average citizen thinks of a historian as someone who knows a lot of facts is probably a consequence of the citizen's own painful experience of being forced by a history teacher to memorize reams of them.

History is something infinitely more complex and more interesting and profoundly more mysterious than facts. As simple "information," history is of little use other than on examinations. In the same way, an individual life is made up of a great number of experiences. The individual learns from these experiences and matures in direct proportion to his or her capacity to reflect on their meaning and absorb into his or her own life their positive consequences.

The study of history is an extension of this process, this act of incorporation. George Santayana wrote that a nation that could not remember its history was doomed to repeat it. In the most extreme cases a person who cannot learn from experience (personal history) is classified as retarded. But this capacity to learn from experience clearly does not rest on mastering "facts." In our own personal histories we have no notion that the validity of a specific experience depends on our remembering the precise date on which it happened or, for that matter, the year. I cannot remember the date of the most moving and disturbing experience of my life: the death of my mother. That may indeed be because, for me, that event exists outside of time. I experience it daily.

A fact is often taken to represent something that has happened and is "over," whereas all true history continues and exists as much in our future as in our past. If the purpose of teaching history were to be defined as *making students aware of the power of history in their own lives* or as *making students conscious of themselves as historical beings*, it would, I believe, enable us to think more clearly about the problem of teaching history. I suspect that a good deal of the moral and spiritual confusion of our day is related to the failure of most people to feel themselves a part of history. Boris Pasternak wrote that man does not die like a dog in a ditch but lives in history. I have long argued that professional historians have performed a prefrontal lobotomy on the historical consciousness of the American people by embalming our past in scholarly monographs read only by other historians. If the historian does not mediate the past to the present, he becomes a luxury society cannot afford.

To put the matter as succinctly as possible: in order to teach history effectively on the elementary and secondary school level, it is necessary to jettison the whole existing schema of academic history and start over with *history as experience*, rather than history as nationalistic propaganda or history as facts. We should observe the simple and increasingly heeded principle of starting not where the teacher is but where the student is.

BRINGING HISTORY TO LIFE

One of the most rewarding exercises that I discovered in my own teaching of history was the pairing off of students, each to write the biography of the other. This utilizes the natural curiosity of the child (or in my instance, the college student). Children ask each other questions they often would not think of asking themselves. Examples: What do your father and mother do for a living? Where did they come from? Where are your grandmother and grandfather, aunts and uncles, cousins? How far back can you trace your ancestors and from what country are they? All those things place us in time and space, in history.

With this kind of incentive, students have often written to relatives who were known to be repositories of family history to collect material about their antecedents. Usually, unless the class is uncommonly homogeneous in background, students make the discovery that a kind of minor congress of nations and races is represented in the classroom itself. Once the biographies have been composed, a resourceful teacher will think of any number of ways to recreate substantial segments of American history out of the materials that the students have collected on each other.

The biography of a Japanese-American student, for example, would provide the teacher with an opportunity to introduce the class to the extraordinary richness and drama of Japanese culture, the nature and reasons for Japanese immigration to the United States, the "relocation" of Japanese-Americans during World War II, and the remarkable rise of Japan since the end of World War II as the most successful industrial nation in the world today.

Another history class might wish to compose a history of its school and by doing so enter quite naturally into the history of education in America (and the world). And, of course, there is an inexhaustible field for neighborhood and local history, in which interviewing older people in the community would be a basic technique. Each month the class might choose an official class historian, a chronicler charged with organizing the work of the class in such a way as to relate the activities of the students to contemporary events of world history. One student or a group of students might be charged with presenting the Arab case to the United Nations Security Council while another offers the case for the Israelis. One segment of historical studies could start with reports by students on evening (or morning) news accounts. The guiding principle is that history is not some abstract piece of information in textbooks but is part of the daily experience of every student.

THE ARTS AND ARTIFACTS AS RESOURCES

Against the notion of history as facts, I propose the alternative notion of history as drama. I found that my students responded enthusiastically to the opportunity to write plays, television scripts, or movies dealing with incidents, characters, events, and themes in American history.

An important resource can be found in historical novels—stories like LeGrand Cannon's *Look to the Mountain* and Conrad Richter's *The Trees*. The historical books written specifically for children (with certain notable exceptions like *Johnny Tremain* by Esther Forbes) seem to me on the whole rather vapid, but I confess my acquaintanceship with them is casual.

Most useful as resources are the original accounts by participants in historical events. How accessible these will be to pupils will depend in part on their maturity and reading level, but certainly teachers should be familiar with such works as *Sally Wister's Journal*, a young Quaker girl's reaction to the American Revolution, and with Christopher Hawkins's account of his adventures on an American privateer during the Revolution. It is not always easy to find a way to present such materials to younger children, but it is enormously rewarding when it works.

Art is also an effective way to introduce students to history. The art of a period can be revealing, but unless it is skillfully presented it can give children a sense of the remoteness of the past—those people in those funny-looking clothes—rather than of its relevance. Paintings, however, have the virtue of solidifying ideas in a striking way. To move from the eighteenth century's emphasis on portraiture, to the landscapes of the romantic era, and then to the domestic interiors of the late nineteenth century is to track the shift from a cool classical mode, with emphasis on the power of distinguished faces (especially the faces of heroes), to the warm landscapes of the Hudson River School, with their lyrical treatment of space, to the interior space of the upper-class family living room. That is a history lesson itself.

Music is essential as a "source" of history, and its range is vast because the differences in the music of various cultures or groups within a culture are so striking. Moreover, music, like drama, is a mode of expression with special potency for young people.

A history class could get an insight into history by taking a walking tour of the different types of buildings in its community, each bearing the imprint of a historical style that in turn epitomized a whole set of historical ideas and assumptions. Such a tour would provide an opportunity to open up the whole fascinating story of the role of the porch and the rocking chair in American history. What function did the porch play in American social history? What was life like when a family sat on the porch on long, hot summer evenings and watched the world go by? And how does such a lifestyle contrast with that of the air-conditioned family huddled in front of the television?

It is essential for a history class to get out of the classroom and into the community. I think it was Marc Bloch who said historians needed stouter boots, the implication being that they should get out of their libraries and studies and onto the ground where history took place. In this same spirit, a history class might try to reconstruct the character of the original settlement of the community by visiting the local graveyard where the names and dates on the headstones could provide clues to the history of the town. And certainly a trip to the community's hall of records to poke among early deeds and wills will uncover substantial amounts of community history.

Artifacts are also important. In a semifacetious vein, I used to give a lecture during my colonial history course in which I introduced what I called "Multisensory Apperceptive Educational Reinforcement." A rehearsed group from the class would sing a Revolutionary song and then get the class to join in. We would distribute Madeira wine, a popular drink in the British colonies, pass around an old powder horn, an eighteenth-century book, and some snuff in a bottle. (These were college students, remember.) The students were thus able to experience history through all of their senses—taste, smell, sound, sight, and touch. Frivolous as it all was, it made, I think, a valid point: history has to be experienced, not simply read about in textbooks. And it can be experienced in a wide variety of ways—sensed, entered into, absorbed.

DEVELOPING A NEW APPROACH

I suspect it is not particularly helpful to be constantly quarreling with the textbook. That may only confuse the student. And obviously, textbooks are going to have to be used for some time to come. But I confess that I can only see them as the enemy, in the sense that they contain the essence of all that is stultifying in our thinking about and teaching of history.

Black students or women or American Indians may see no relation between the events described in the textbook and the experience of their own race or sex or ethnic group. In a certain sense, of course, the black, the female, and the Indian were not supposed to see any connection. The text was, in a manner of speaking, a coercive instrument designed to force the consciousness of the dominant group on subordinate ones. Having now witnessed the inclusion of such groups in history texts as a consequence, primarily, of their insistence on being included, we should have a considerable degree of skepticism about the claims of the conventional textbook to be a satisfactory account of "what happened."

What textbooks need is to be decontaminated by substantial infusions of imaginative teaching. It is up to the teacher of history, I believe, to beguile the students into entering the magic realm of history by giving them a sense of their reality as historical creatures, by implanting in their brains some modest seed of historical consciousness. This, of course, has little to do with the memorization of dates or battles. I would rather produce a student who looked at the world every day with a sense of the extraordinary richness of historical texture that underlies it than one who knew ten thousand dead facts.

I am aware, of course, that such an approach will and does encounter resistance. What, for instance, about the standardized tests that students have to take based on the oppressive and obsolete conception of history as memorized facts? Considerable patience, tact, and education will be required on the part of teachers, administrators, school boards, as well as the various ubiquitous arbiters of educational processes, if a new mode of teaching history is to emerge. But a start has to be made somewhere, and risks have to be taken, as I'm sure they already have been by enterprising teachers. So I would say with Admiral Perry (or was it Farragut?): "Damn the torpedoes! Full speed ahead."

The Lost Art
1954 of Declamation

I inhaled deeply and began:

> Breathes there the man, with soul so dead,
> Who never to himself hath said,
> This is my own, my native land . . .

Accompanying the words with suitable gestures, I came at length to
the finale: "If such there breathe," the unpatriotic wretch, "living,
shall forfeit fair renown / And, doubly dying (whatever kind of dying
that is) shall go down / To the vile dust from whence he sprung, / Un-
wept, unhonored and unsung."

I finished, somewhat flushed and breathless, but pleased with the effect of the florid words on my classmates.

In Miss Van Vlack's fourth-grade class at the Gilman Country School
some thirty years ago we learned such sonorous verses by the yard.

If you mention memorizing to a present-day pedagogue, he turns
pale. When he has recovered his equilibrium, he explains patiently, as
to a retarded child, that memorizing is an obsolete, outmoded way of
learning. We "learn in context," we "learn by doing," we "learn by observing how things work, not by sterile definitions," etc. Memory work,
it seems, damages youthful noggins and warps immature personalities.

Fortunately, Miss Van Vlack and her colleagues were unaware of
such doctrines, so we all recited away quite happily, and much acquired
then and in subsequent years remains a pleasant resource. Indeed, I

never see a bleak winter sky that I do not recall the lines from "Snow-bound":

> The sun that brief December day
> Rose cheerless over hills of gray,
> And, darkly circled, gave at noon
> A sadder light than waning moon.
> Slow tracing down the thickening sky
> Its mute and ominous prophecy,

We especially liked, as I recall, the more morbid poems dealing with death and untimely demise. We were prepared to go with Bryant:

> . . . not, like the guarry-slave at
>   night,
> Scourged to his dungeon, but,
>   sustained and soothed,
> By an unfaltering trust, approach
>   thy grave
> Like one who wraps the drapery
>   of his couch
> About him, and lies down to
>   pleasant dreams.

In addition to memorizing a sizable number of poems and a good deal of Shakespeare, we learned much prose. In doing so we partook of an older tradition represented by the McGuffey Readers. These noble books contained dozens of great set pieces from America's past—such things as the Declaration of Independence, Washington's Farewell Address, Patrick Henry's "Give Me Liberty or Give Me Death," the Gettysburg Address, and, one of the most famous, Chief Logan's speech to Lord Dunmore after his family had been murdered by renegade whites. That eloquent redskin is reported to have expressed himself thus:

"I appeal to any white man to say, if ever he entered Logan's cabin hungry, and he gave him not meat; if ever he came cold and naked and he clothed him not."

This friendship had been rewarded by perfidy, and Logan in turn had "killed man" and "fully glutted" his vengeance. He now accepted it in fear.

"Logan never felt fear. He will not turn on his heel to save his life. Who is there to mourn for Logan? Not one."

The speech expressed much of the tragedy of the American savage, and many schoolboys as they recited the classic lines doubtless felt its stoic dignity and resignation.

Such exercises gave the pupil contact with the great figures and the great epochs of the past. Reciting before the class, he experienced vicariously the heroic episodes, became himself Horatius at the bridge, Mark Antony orating over the bier of his fallen chief, Henry V at Agincourt, Patrick Henry defying tyranny. Words thus committed to memory echoed in the inner consciousness. They constituted dramatic embodiment of those old-fashioned oddities—moral values.

Beyond such classic utterances of the human spirit in prose and poetry in the classroom, we engaged also, in those distant years, in declamations. These were contests in which (in opposition to modern educational theory) some lost and some won. Here pint-sized declaimers strove earnestly to outdo each other. And here, it may be said, Kipling was a godsend: "Recessional," "Fuzzy-Wuzzy" ("with your 'ayrick 'ead of 'air"), and, best of all, "Gunga Din."

Why, I can still hold a dinner party spellbound with my dramatic rendition of the Kipling epic delivered in a kind of throttled pseudo-cockney, and ending:

> So I'll meet 'im later on
> At the place where 'e
>   'is gone—
> Where it's always double
>   drill and no canteen.
> 'E'll be squattin' on the coals
> Givin' drinks to poor
>   damned souls,
> An' I'll get a swig in hell
>   from Gunga Din!

Surely, a grand vision!

"The Charge of the Light Brigade" was another favorite in declamations and of course Robert Burns, whose democratic rural sentiments ("a man's a man for a' that") endeared him to countless rustic youths. The actor, Dean Jagger, recalls how, as a farm boy, he plowed with a copy of Burns's poems in his hand, memorizing them as he tramped the new-turned furrows.

We are too enlightened today to bother with such dusty customs of the past as memorization. We pride ourselves on having freed the child's mind from tedious learning by rote. And so we deprive our children of one of the purest pleasures of learning.

What the educational psychologists have overlooked, of course, in their progressive wisdom is that children enjoy memorizing. Memorizing something of eloquence or beauty not infrequently gives a child a deep sense of accomplishment. Moreover, it provides a most desirable training in diction and enunciation, develops a sense of style, and encourages a feeling for the nuances of words—in all of which contemporary education is conspicuously weak.

I am bone-tired of the modern cant about learning skills, reading skills, language skills. A bleak world, this world of skills. We need to revitalize our education with some of the classics of our literary and political—or, in the larger sense, our spiritual and moral heritage, and I suggest that a good place to start would be with memorization.

By restoring memory work to an honored place in our curriculum, we will take a necessary step in recovering a genuine insight into our past, we will repair those "mystic cords of memory" of which Lincoln spoke. Enriching our individual memories, we will strengthen that collective memory which knits us together in our common humanity. Thus we will have truly "enriched" the curriculum.

The Universal
1976 Curriculum

I suspect it could be shown (and probably has been) that all systems of education from the tribe to far more complex civilizations have grown out of and rested upon the religious beliefs of the societies of which such systems or principles were a part. That is to say, whether we are talking about the initiation rights of a simple nomadic people or about the great universities of the Arabic or Western World, all "educational" ventures have been originally conceived of as a means of discovering and stating the ultimate truths which gave order, coherence, and meaning to a particular society. Education was not something "for the individual" but the passing on of values and attitudes deemed essential by the society. It was not the disinterested "pursuit of truth"; it was the means of survival.

The Reformation, as derived from Calvin, was the basis of education in America: to know and to do God's will, to know God's will by reason and revelation unclouded by ignorance and superstition.

It followed that the curriculum was shaped and given its purpose by these ultimate ends. The community could not escape worldliness and corruption unless the young were taught those truths which confirmed and authenticated the society. The actual content of the curriculum was incidental. Or, to put it another way, the curriculum was simply the bearer of the community's values.

By the end of the nineteenth century the curriculum had become secularized. It had broken away from its origins in Reformed Christianity and been established as a separate, independent value, as a procedure by which people were *trained* in *skills* and *techniques*. Values of course still dominated the curriculum, but they were now practical, secular values: good citizenship, getting ahead, Americanism, and so on. The system of primary and secondary education, moreover, had so much momentum that it carried its subjects—the pupils—along with it for several generations. In the face of waves of immigration it also performed a vitally important socializing role, but it appears in retrospect that the assumptions on which it had originally been based withered away and were replaced in rather random fashion by an odd amalgam of ideas, values, and practices that had very little coherence.

All of this is familiar enough. It seems increasingly clear that the basic institutions of contemporary American society are in an advanced state of demoralization and, perhaps, of disintegration. Education is one of those institutions and it is obviously suffering from the same disease that has affected all other institutions.

This abbreviated tour of the educational scene, past and present, brings me to a question first posed by my colleague, Norman O. Brown: Is a secular education possible? If, as we have suggested, all methods, procedures, or systems of education have had their origin in the religious doctrines of a society, one is inclined to speculate at least that secularization must bring with it disenchantment and confusion about the real nature and purpose of education. From this proposition follows two obvious conclusions. One is that we have reached a new stage in human development where reason unencumbered by superstition (religion) is able to take over and guide society. Thus what seems, or at least is argued here, to have been true in the past—the primacy of religious values in education—need (and should) no longer be true. This proposition is, in fact, the one that has dominated the educational scene since the latter decades of the nineteenth century. Perhaps it is the only option available to a "pluralistic" society. Be that as it may, it is plain enough that American education is at present in a sad muddle.

The other conclusion is, of course, that any genuine education is impossible in this particular era and that we have no choice but to struggle along until some new "order" with a new or renewed set of religious imperatives emerges in the name of which education can be once more given direction, order, and coherence.

Another possibility, however, is that there is still largely unexplored territory between "knowledge" and "skills"—between essential truths and simple mechanics—and that this territory needs to be mapped.

At this point two further things need to be said. One is that education is a process that cannot be separated into stages called "elementary school," "secondary school," and "college" or "higher education." A large part of our problem stems from the fact that we insist on talking about these three parts of a single process as though they were independent entities. Thus we speak about the reform of higher education, secondary education, primary education, as though these were autonomous or semiautonomous entities (as, unfortunately, they seem to be in our society). And different people talk about the reform of these different entities. Until we all talk about the reform of education as a single continuous process, we will get nowhere. Subjecting students to three separate kinds of sequential educational experience, each dominated by a different philosophy, is clearly preposterous.

The second point I wish to make is that the American university as we know it today took shape in the period after the secularization of education. It thus embodied secularism in an extreme form. Where important residues of the earlier religiously oriented education lingered on in the atmosphere if not the curriculum of elementary and secondary schools (represented by such notions as making "good citizens" of the students), the college and university became centers of "value-free," "scientific" research and teaching. Any possible coherence was destroyed by innumerable specialized "courses" that were presented as containing the truth or truths—now scientific and scholarly rather than religious—of a particular field or discipline. The new dogmatism was as rigid as the old, and what is more it was disintegrative rather than unifying—a thousand independent dogmas instead of one. The shift was, among other things, from morality to what we might call "operationalism," from what was right to how things worked.

The only problem was, as it turned out, things didn't work that way. Outside of the area of "natural sciences" the new, value-free, scientific scholarship proved, if anything, less capable of explaining and shaping the world of human beings than the old humanistic-religious scholarship.

What I wish to emphasize is that the domination of our common intellectual life by the colleges and universities with their "system of orthodoxies," as rigid as those of any religious zealots, affected every level of the educational experience in the United States. What thus developed was, in fact, a highly segmented educational "system" or nonsystem that was held together, not by a dominant philosophy directed toward certain clearly perceived and generally agreed upon goals but a nightmare of often conflicting philosophies and assumptions. Elementary school became increasingly preoccupied with shaping a "creative individual," the secondary school avowed its intention of producing a "good citizen" (which more and more gave way under the pressure of higher education to preparing students to be admitted to the college or university). The university, or multiversity, prided itself on disinterested, objective scholarship, on advancing "the frontiers of knowledge," or on serving the practical needs of the larger society for trained experts in a wide variety of fields.

It was thus in the area of higher education that the disintegration of traditional values proceeded at the most rapid rate. Along with their system of orthodoxies, the colleges and universities (the universities were the real culprits, the colleges tagged along behind for the most part) exercised absolute tyranny over secondary education by prescribing what high school students must study (and how they must study it) in order to be admitted to college.

Put another way, the specialized graduate education developed by the universities determined the nature of undergraduate education (segments of specialized knowledge encapsulated in "courses"). Undergraduate education became, increasingly, a by-product of graduate education (and a generally neglected by-product). The nature of undergraduate education determined the nature of secondary education, while elementary education turned increasingly into a kind of playground where, it was hoped, a "creativity" might be planted in the students that was strong enough to resist the debilitating effects of the arid zones ahead.

It is necessary to state these propositions in order to even begin to talk about the reform of education on all levels.

Leaving aside for the time being the question of whether the assertions are true, let us consider what might follow from them if they are.

We must agree, for example, that reform of education should start from the bottom rather than be dominated from the top. I believe graduate education to be so thoroughly discredited at this moment that we can safely turn our backs on it. Thus we can free ourselves of the notion, stated or unstated, that the goal of "lower" education is to prepare students, ultimately and ideally, for graduate school. Next we can ask ourselves what do we, inhabitants of the United States, need to know in order to exist in a modern industrial, technological society? How, for example, can we become reasonably independent once more? Interdependent we must be but wholly dependent we need not be.

The second question I would pose is: Assuming we cannot tolerate an educational process devoid of any "ordering principle," what principle of order can we discover around which a so-called curriculum can be constructed? Ideally, this principle of order should be one that can start in first grade (or kindergarten).

Ideally, again, it would be a religious principle, that is, to know and serve God better. But since that is manifestly impossible, we must find some other "principle of order." I propose one such principle; certainly there must be others. My principle is based on the need to bring education at once to the most direct and practical concerns of our daily life. Therefore, I would establish the study of law and medicine as the "ordering principles" of my educational system. My reasons are as follows. Law and medicine are continuous experiences, that is, the individuals are acted upon and act through law and medicine from their earliest consciousness. Law is simply the principle that there must be order in human groups from the family outward to nations. Law is experienced by the child in a family, by the citizen in his community. It comprehends politics (the means by which law is enacted), society, theology, economy, even, if you will, psychology—all the social studies. It appears, perhaps most strikingly, in the area of the dramatic arts. The study of law is thus both practical and the most abstract and theoretical kind of study. It is, therefore, ideally suited to be taught progressively, that is, according to the development of the understanding and intellectual sophistication of the student, from the first grade through the last, whatever the last may be. The study of morality and ethics is, of course, an essential part of the law, not to mention history and anthropology. Through the study of law, abstract problems are rendered practical and comprehensible, and practical problems are lifted out of the realm of the mundane and related to larger human issues.

With medicine the case is much the same. At certain points indeed law and medicine intersect. Young children are preoccupied with their bodies. Typically, they wish to play "doctor" as a cover for this developing interest. Medicine is the human science that includes biology and psychology, chemistry and physics. By studying all these subjects as they relate to medicine (that is to say to the health of the human organism) their conventional treatment as separate disciplines is overcome and many of the ethical problems connected with certain fields of scientific investigation (such as genetics) are, if not entirely avoided, at least brought within a specifically human frame of reference.

Another reason to make law and medicine the ordering principles of a new system of education is that both these great studies have been sadly abused in our era by their practitioners. Law (as witness Watergate) has been corrupted by being placed at the service of those willing to pay preposterous prices to have use of it for selfish purposes. Medicine has enriched its practitioners at the expense of their patients and is on the verge of becoming a nightmare for low-income Americans. Like law, it must be reformed for the good of the society. That is not, of course, the reason for placing law and medicine at the center of the new curriculum. They can be justified in their own terms. But it is certainly true that we must free ourselves of the tyranny of these overprofessionalized fields.

With law and medicine as the central disciplines of the curriculum, the rest can be highly unstructured. If independence from a technological society is a proper aim, a number of other subjects present themselves at once—motor mechanics and electrical engineering, plumbing and carpentry, horticulture, animal husbandry, elementary aeronautics, seamanship, communications, mountain and wilderness training.

Then, finally, there are the most important studies of all—the life-enhancing studies—dance, music, drama, pottery, painting, sculpture, architecture, arithmetic, storytelling, poetry.

In the new curriculum there are perhaps no school buildings at all.

Or a complex of buildings used by five different schools on five different days. Education without walls or with a bare minimum of technical facilities—laboratories, studios, and so on, *must* come. Most of the education under the universal curriculum will take place in the community in which the student lives and without benefit of courses and credits. Old people, middle-aged people, young people, and children are all involved together in the educational process.

While law and medicine have "a curriculum," students master it at their own pace. In most of the other subjects, students learn the rudiments and then continue or not as their interests and talents dictate.

The Universal Curriculum would seem wildly Utopian were it not for two facts: education is becoming ruinously expensive in the United States, and fewer and fewer people—students, teachers, or parents—feel that its accomplishments are worth its cost.

As to the question of whether the Universal Curriculum is presented as a serious alternative to the present unwieldy and deeply entrenched system of public education in the United States, I can only say that it is at least a point from which the existing system can be viewed and criticized; it thus serves as a means of engaging the subject. But beyond that, I believe that the Universal Curriculum could be easily and inexpensively initiated on an experimental basis. Only then could one begin to speak with confidence about whether it (or any other) curriculum can withstand the general intellectual and moral confusion of this period of history.

It seems not unreasonable to ask: In an ideal society, what would be the social role of education? I have no truck with ideal societies, but it should be clear by now that I believe that in healthy and vigorous societies the "social role" of education is to teach what in the view of the society *must be learned* in order for the society to survive. The *must be learned* is crucial here (as opposed to what *may* be learned, what is interesting to learn, what leads to self-expression, creativity, and so on. The real issue is the imperative, the *must*. Since the ultimate ends of a society have traditionally been expressed in its religion (belief system, I suppose, would be the modern jargon), that would seem to take care of the matter of "moral education," but we clearly cannot acquire that comprehensive religious faith that would give coherence to our education by wishing for it. Therefore, we must do the next best thing and seek, as we have said, "a principle of order" as representing at least a common goal and a substantial measure of unity. The moral issues will, of course, reassert themselves once we have stopped trying to exclude them in the name of value-free science.

One thing further may be said. Any new vision of education must be, in its essence, international. It should not be filled with pious observations about universal brotherhood (nor need it or should it be hostile to or neglectful of one's own national tradition); it should take for granted that we are all part of an international community in the process of becoming, and everything taught should be taught from that perspective.

Part Three

The Editorial Eye

Confessions
1956 of a Twelve
O'Clock Scholar

On several occasions recently I have found myself saying in a weighty professorial manner, "Yes, what we need is more emphasis on the fundamentals in high schools. More rigor. We must weed out the weak sisters; raise the standards; insist that students study mathematics, physics, Latin, and French."

Yet I falter in my pronouncements as I hear a mocking inner voice ask, "And how would you have fared under such a regimen, professor?"

The truth is my youth was spent in a prolonged warfare against all the academic proprieties. It was not the resistance of a precocious and imaginative child to dull routines. It was the resistance of a vague and lazy child to dull routines. By dint of frequent tutoring and continual parental prodding I finally advanced, reluctantly, to the fifth grade, where I rested for two years.

Almost wholly impervious to learning, I became a kind of proving ground for fledgling pedagogues. Those who could teach me something were considered equal to any challenge the profession could offer.

My mother, who was as determined that I should be educated as I was to resist the process, once sent me off to a summer tutoring school in New York State, presumably away from all distracting influences, where I could receive the combined attention of a skilled staff, especially trained in cramming knowledge into the craniums of obtuse youths.

So I progressed, pushed and pulled from grade to grade, dropping Latin for German and German for French in an effort to find a foreign language whose rudiments I could penetrate. Spending two years (and several summers) in the unfathomable mysteries of plain geometry and wringing from one harassed teacher the (as it came to be) classic observation that I was "a pretty blank Page."

At only one thing did I excel—talking. I was the luminary of the public-speaking class and the debating society. On every subject I was ready to speak at length.

I left school diplomaless but with a handsome cup for orating, and I fancied that as I departed I heard a vast sigh of relief. Barred from Princeton (where all good young Baltimoreans hope to go when they graduate) by my failure to pass that Cerberus, the college boards, I managed to slip into a respectable New England college through a gap in the admissions policy.

I departed for the North without much hope of academic survival, determined to get in some trout fishing and grouse hunting before I was "sent down." I never did get around to fishing. Distracted by some teachers and some courses and encouraged by the discovery of the random joys of the elective system, I hung around long enough to collect a B. A. Indeed, I even collected a retroactive high school diploma.

One of the main themes of my youth was an untiring warfare with my grandmother, who objected to my general shiftlessness, which, to her, was expressed in the constant reading of books of dubious merit and morals. She thus bent a large part of her considerable energies to preventing my reading in the name of more manly and more practical endeavors. I, showing the same patient guile that I employed to evade schoolwork, read in stray corners, behind sofas, in the stable, in closets by flashlight, or wherever I could find a brief refuge. I won the war at last, but my grandmother's triumph was to give me the subconscious feeling that reading was a wicked evasion of serious responsibilities.

When it occurred to me that I might, by combining my pleasure in talking with my delight in reading, become a college professor and thus live in a perpetual state of wickedness and be paid for it, I do not recall. But once the notion struck me I became a dedicated man.

The acquisition of a higher degree in America requires today primarily patience, a patience that is often hardly to be distinguished from inertia. Such qualities I had in abundance and so, I am sure to the vast amusement of the gods and the amazement of my boyhood mentors, I became a registered, certified egghead. From this pinnacle I can say, with professorial solemnity, to anyone who is unfamiliar with my disreputable academic past, "Let's not waste time with these dullards who can't keep up! No time for loafers! Raise the standards!"

And I believe it.

The Vanishing
1955 Gentleman

The Vanishing American is not, it seems, vanishing at all. On the contrary, I understand that the native Indian population within the United States has been increasing for some time, and ethnologists speculate that there may be more Indians in this country today than there were when John Smith engaged in noggin knocking with Chief Powhatan.

The title having been, so to speak, declared vacant, I have a nominee of my own.

The real Vanishing American is, I submit, the Gentleman. There are, of course, a few still left, but most of them would be frightfully embarrassed to be identified as such.

To be called a gentleman is, to be sure, still not quite as disapprobatory as to be called a Communist, but it's no help. (I know of one unhappy wretch who, seeking an academic position, was referred to in a letter of recommendation as a "gentleman." When this was read aloud to the group considering his appointment it occasioned much merriment and almost cost him the job. The rest of his credentials being respectable, however, the flaw was overlooked; he was hired and proved in fact to be not a gentleman at all but a very decent sort of fellow.)

But I was raised to be one. Growing up in the home of my thoroughly Victorian grandparents, I was daily exhorted to be a gentleman. And I suppose I might thus claim to have been an apprentice gentleman or a novice of the order.

Moreover, as I look back on the canons of a gentleman, it seems to me that they had a good deal to recommend them. Courtesy, of course, was of first importance, not etiquette. That was for those who confused minor social forms with the larger ideal. A gentleman, to be sure, rose when ladies entered the room, gave up his seat on public conveyances, tipped his hat, removed it in elevators, and in general treated the opposite sex with gentleness and consideration.

But these were not the important canons. Those had to do with a sense of responsibility, of personal worth and dignity (not pride or arrogance), and with the proper performance of one's duties, which were manifold. To me, as a boy, they seemed endless.

A gentleman, my grandparents sought to impress upon me, did not push himself forward at the expense of others, or advertise himself, or curry favor, did not stoop to small chicane, did not connive or cheat. These were foremost among the things that were "simply not done."

A gentleman, ideally, was modest and self-effacing. He was always polite but he did not feign an immediate, overwhelming, back-slapping affection for someone he had just met. He kept some of himself in reserve and did not display all his forces at the first encounter.

Although he liked to live well he avoided like the plague vulgar display and ostentation. He honored intelligence and courage—indeed all those qualities that used to be spoken of collectively as character.

There was no confusion of values. There was also a minimum of self-consciousness because one's eyes were fixed on the ideal image rather than on one's own psyche. The gentleman was not concerned about the judgments of "the group." He didn't give a hang or a hoop for the group. He was confident that his own personal standards, the standards of a gentleman, were unimpeachable.

It did not, for instance, occur to a gentleman to abandon the ladies in a distant corner of the room while he discussed with his fellows the state of the market or the price of steel. He knew that it was bad taste to carry business concerns into social discourse.

My grandfather was a gentleman, not a perfect one, to be sure (there are none), but a reasonably good and, to me, a thoroughly impressive one. So were my uncles. But I came along too late. Despite their example, I succumbed to "good guyism."

So perhaps it is a bad conscience that makes me look back nostalgically to the ideal, if infrequently realized, image of the gentleman. I have no doubt myself that we would have a better, truer, and more honest society were every Common Man a gentleman. And, of course, in a democracy that is entirely possible.

It took Sputniks I and II to arouse us, in a near panic, to some of the shortcomings of our educational system as compared with that of the Russians (I think, incidentally, that these shortcomings have been somewhat exaggerated). It would be a fine kind of irony if we were to discover someday that the Russians had reconstituted the gentleman (under an assumed Marxist name, of course). Then no doubt we should rush around appropriating vast sums of money and launching huge government projects to create gentlemen once more.

But then, I fear, it will be too late. The type will be extinct. The Vanishing American will have vanished and we will all be social aborigines.

Nurses

and Nannies

The author of *"Where Did You Go?" "Out." "What Did You Do?"* *"Nothing,"* besides having a great title, has a good point. Opportunities for the kind of casual unsupervised adventures traditionally dear to the hearts of American boys have, today, largely disappeared.

Another classic component of early childhood that has vanished is the nurse—the "Nanny" of nineteenth-century English children's literature. (I have virtually given up reading this class of juvenilia to my children because they are persistently baffled by the omnipresent Nanny.)

This once ubiquitous female is now as rare as the duck-billed platypus and as difficult and expensive to keep. A generation ago you could employ a tough, seasoned trooper of a nurse more familiar with the wiles and foibles of small fry than a child psychologist for far less than you pay today for a pin-curled, blue-jeaned, rock-and-roll-crazed baby sitter only a few years out of diapers herself.

I regret the passing of the breed and recall with pleasure some of those into whose hands I was delivered.

Madame C was a timid Frenchwoman who took me over when I was approximately three and communicated to me a whole inventory of expressive Gallic fears and (to accompany them) French exclamations. I soon spoke more French than English though my vocabulary was limited primarily to words and phrases of alarm and apprehension. "Voilà!" I would cry. "Regardez le chien terrible!" Or "le crasseux charbon," or whatever it might be that had filled Madame with terror or disgust.

My relationship with Madame C ended when I closed a closet door while she was in the closet. My mother, out at the time, returned to our hotel room an hour later to find the poor woman half dead of fright and exhaustion. "That cheeld," she cried, "he haf tried to keel me."

My nurses undoubtedly found conditions of employment difficult. In addition to my persistent if inexperienced efforts to do them in, they had to contend with my grandmother, who believed firmly in original sin and suspected them all of secret vices.

Grandmother felt completely vindicated when, after several years of patient sleuthing, she finally apprehended one who made a practice of drinking the cream from the top of the bottle and giving me the skimmed milk. This wicked woman was at once discharged, joining thereby a rapidly growing company of former nurses of mine.

The nurse I remember most distinctly was not my own. She was the nurse of a female cousin several years my junior with whom I went often to play. An autocratic, snappish woman, heavily powdered and tightly corseted, she was more than a match for my juvenile cunning. Her starched, threatening bulk loomed over us like a dark shadow and her sharp eyes nipped dozens of promising projects in the bud.

My cousin, a gentle, carefully nurtured child, had a tired, harassed white mouse which in the cruel and depraved way of small children we tormented as much as we dared.

Gradually the idea of bringing mouse and nurse into some kind of a wild harmony possessed me. Drawing my innocent cousin into the plot, I took Albert by the tail and tracked Nurse to the kitchen, where in an unguarded moment she was eating a buttered crumpet and reading the society page of the *Baltimore Sun*. As stealthily as an Indian scout I crept up behind her and then, in the moment of truth, dropped the terrified rodent down the back of her dress where (as I later learned) it lodged in her corset.

The results of this happy conjuncture were (and remain) indescribable. An enormous and explosive symphony of sound and motion at once took place before my dazzled and horrified eyes. In the moment before I fled, I saw this large, unwieldy woman rise, gyrate, revolve as in the convolutions of a barbaric dance, emitting screams of more than gratifying pitch and volume.

Then, delighted and terrified, I ran from the retribution that I knew must finally overtake me.

It was a year and several nurses later before I was permitted in my cousin's house again. My reputation had preceded me and the incumbent nurse regarded me much as I imagine she would have regarded a rattlesnake—as an enemy of mankind. But I returned a chastened and tractable child. I suppose I perceived, dimly, that in life between the conception and the achievement falls, generally, a shadow and that there was in this classic juxtaposition of mouse and nurse a kind of perfection that I would never attain again.

But the episode left me with an affection for children's nurses (as an institution) that still lingers. There are none left today to speak of and I am sure the lives of enterprising little boys and girls are duller as a consequence. They have only their parents to war against. And as any child knows, parents are patsies.

Home,

Sweet Home

Abigail Adams used to complain to John that he and his colleagues in the Continental Congress talked glibly enough of liberty but failed to extend its benefits to their own wives. The charge has been often repeated, never more frequently than at present.

The misguided male (if indeed it was a male) who first said, "A woman's place is in the home," saddled us all, men and women alike, with a disastrous legacy. The effect of using the home to symbolize women's inferior status—at least in an industrial society where men go away to do the presumably "important" money-making work—was to make escape from the home the symbol of women's liberation. This gets everything wrong.

Perhaps the most negative aspect of contemporary American society is the quality of work. Most of us work within large institutional structures, often in vast impersonal buildings that are aesthetically sterile and emotionally alienating. We have far too little control over our work, over our lives, over our total "environment"—psychological as well as physical.

We travel over energy-draining freeways to work in "factories" (even though we may call them universities or offices) where we have little sense of the usefulness of our labor, where we waste extraordinary amounts of time, where we constantly have to contend with "interpersonal" relationships and struggle with problems of "communication," where we have to experience the corrosive effects of rivalry, ambition, anxiety, and, usually, powerlessness. We are objects in an artificial landscape not of our own devising.

There is only one environment, in fact, where most of us have any control at all—our home. There *we* create the environment and set the tone. It is, or should be, or can be, the one place where we enact the drama of our own reality, where we are ourselves, free of those debilitating distortions of reality that most of us experience at our "work."

The flight from home is thus a flight from ourselves—from our own barrenness, inattention, unimaginativeness, unlovingness—to the spiritually numbing distraction of most jobs and careers, to a world of ceaseless motion, restlessness, misplaced ardor, false hopes, all the illusions of power and success of which our culture is so prolific.

Today, nevertheless, the home—which should be a center of peace and joy, of the classic domestic delights that have sustained life for centuries—is depicted as a prison cell, the abode of a boredom only slightly relieved by the pale blue flicker of television or, more commonly perhaps, as a bedlam of squabbling children, unmade beds, and unwashed dishes, presided over by a mad housewife, tranquilized twice daily, tending to dipsomania.

I would reiterate an old saw: There is nothing in the world as enthralling as the process by which an infant grows into an adult. Raising a child is often exhausting, but it is also the profoundest experience of our own humanity. In seeing our children grow up, we rehumanize ourselves, an occurrence surely of crucial importance in a society so ingenious in dehumanizing us. If we cannot stand the arduousness of parenthood while enjoying its unique pleasures, then we should not marry and beget or, at any rate, we should not beget.

We certainly delude ourselves if we think that an environment exists "outside" that is infinitely more alluring than the home, with or without children. If we make the home no more than a convenient station—a bed, bath, and kitchen (full, no doubt, of frozen dinners) in which to recuperate briefly from the excitement and stimulations of the outside world—then we simply give up by far the better part of all that enhances life; we become savages in the modern urban jungle. No, not savages even, for the family is everything to them; rather we become frightened animals living in sky-high burrows, fearing the next knock on the door.

I don't want to "condemn" anyone to the home, man or woman. But

I have a settled conviction that a man's and a woman's place is in the home. I have spent as much of my life in mine as I could. I leave it reluctantly; I return to it joyfully. I can hardly persuade my wife to leave it at all.

She has made it into such a splendid refuge, such a magnificent nest resplendent with visual treasures, with aesthetic delights, with surprises, joys, comforts, as can hardly be imagined. The most ingenious and beneficent employer, lavish as Croesus, could not do a tenth as well.

Dear women's liberationists, I wished your liberation before many of you felt yourselves enslaved. I wish you every good thing in the world. If desperate necessity drives you to work, I wish you work more interesting and rewarding than that most men engage in—and certainly equal pay and equal opportunities.

But desist, I beg you, from denigrating the home. That is where I live and where, I trust, you live. I wish you, as the best legacy of all, its joys and delights.

Do not depict the home as the prison to escape from, for you will find that your home is you—as surely as it is your husband and your children—and none of us can escape, finally, from ourselves.

Fidelity

I had a talk with a young friend not long ago in which the conversation turned to some of my former students, mutual friends of ours, whose marriages had ended in divorce or separation.

Thereupon, I indulged myself in some reflections about divorces among friends of my generation (I am fifty-seven). These were rare, comparatively speaking. More frequent have been the divorces among friends a decade or so younger, and there seems to be a pattern.

In a number of cases, wives abandoned bewildered husbands to "find themselves" or "express themselves" or prove that they were "not merely housewives and mothers."

Where husbands initiated the divorce, most commonly they found irresistible the sudden popularity of middle-aged males among young women in their late teens and twenties. The forties and, even more, the fifties are a time when most men begin to be painfully conscious of the aging process and of their own mortality.

Girls, or young women, are and probably always have been conspicuous figures in middle-aged masculine fantasies. Lately they have become available—quite literally—to those same middle-aged fantasists. Just what the mechanics of this process are remain obscure. It seems compounded of at least four elements:

• Many middle-aged men are, in fact, physically attractive (perhaps this is just another of *my* middle-aged fantasies).

• Intellectually and financially (and less often, I suspect, emotionally), these middle-aged males may appear to young women as rewarding alternatives to the callow youths close at hand with whose fragile psyches, immaturities, and insecurities they are already thoroughly familiar.

• The disappearance of sexual inhibitions (and conventional notions of morality) means that all relationships suddenly become possible. The threat of scandal that once helped to keep middle-aged fantasies simply fantasies has greatly diminished. *Why not do whatever one wishes to do?*

• Finally, one senses doomsday psychology in the land—a psychology which, it might be argued, characterizes societies that are in a process of disintegration, for it expresses itself in a frantic pursuit of sensation, of pleasure, or of mere titillation, to escape a terrible, consuming boredom with one's self, with one's surroundings (of which one's wife is a part), with one's job, friends, lifestyle, whatever.

When I had delivered myself of these lugubrious reflections (doubtless putting rather more emphasis on the wife seeking to find herself than the husband in search of perpetual youth), my young friend, who had listened politely, noted that few if any of these explanations were relevant to the divorces among her contemporaries. She was speaking, for the most part, of the young men and women who had entered graduate school at the same time she had, couples with whom she had common interests, similar careers, shared values.

The women were not household drudges, confined to the kitchens (a largely mythical species in my experience). Nor were the men obsessed by a sense of diminishing powers. What then was the problem? What marriages could have more going for them?

My friend's opinion was that 80 percent of the broken marriages came apart primarily because they were "open." That is to say that these couples, before they got married—which was often not much more than a concession to convention and convenience—solemnly agreed not to be "possessive" of one another.

To be nonpossessive was to be open, progressive, modern, enlightened—free. The most crucial test of nonpossessiveness was in the matter of sexual relations.

Both members of the marriage were supposed to enjoy sex with whomever one liked and enjoyed and "related to" at the moment. Yet, I was told, it was the inability of those young married couples to live with the consequences of such high-minded (and simple-minded) commitments that had wrecked their marriages. Strange old things like guilt and possessiveness and disappointment and humiliation, not to mention loneliness and sense of betrayal, rose up to haunt them in their modern, enlightened wisdom.

My young friend may or may not have been correct in her analysis. Certainly she knows far more of such matters than I do, but as I listened to her I was reminded of how much we are the victims of ideas. So much of what happens to us is the consequence of ideas that have been embedded in our funny little brains. When the notion of fidelity was lodged there, we were reasonably faithful, mate to mate; at least we tried our best and stuck it out, the good and the bad, and often we grew old and loving and somewhat wise in the process.

Nowadays, with a quite different set of ideas firmly implanted in our brains, some of us have come to believe more in "openness" than in that odd, obsolete notion of—yes, fidelity.

Nevertheless, for all our couplings and uncouplings and comings and goings, all our fine freedoms and liberations, I haven't noticed that we come out any healthier, wiser, kinder, more generous, or, above all, any happier. (If we did, it would be hard to argue with the new ethic.)

It was in this way, listening to my friend, that I decided I would like to say a good word for fidelity. Somewhere someone might hear it and take heart; it might stir some ancient memory or lodge in some brain with a little space left for a startling new idea.

Fidelity is made up of mutual belonging. Of belonging to each other. It is composed of the ties of affection and selflessness that allow us to enter deeply and tenderly into another's life, that precious kingdom so desperately vulnerable to indifference and cruelty. How else do we learn another's nature (and our own) but by patience and care and time?

For as long as I can remember, I have wished, I suppose above all else, to belong to someone and to have someone who belonged to me. I'm afraid I lack the courage, moral hardihood, or resolution to go it alone, to be an "autonomous" human being. I need all the support I can get from my wife, my friends, my children, all those I love and who, I trust, love me—all those I belong to and who belong to me.

Fidelity is an act, not simply an expression or an avowal. One does not become faithful by taking a marriage vow; one becomes faithful by adhering to principle or, more important, to a person.

Fidelity requires an exclusive attachment to another, for promiscuity and faithfulness are at eternal war with each other. Sex is a secondary issue. To refrain from sexual relations with someone other than one's wife is only important as a direct, practical way of making fidelity evident. It is a way of expressing respect for everything that has been nurtured carefully—often painfully—in two lives committed to each other.

The ramifications of the notion of fidelity are virtually limitless. Indeed, given the prevailing climate, we need a philosophy of fidelity and philosophers of it as well. We need to have it demonstrated in terms difficult to evade, that without fidelity one does not become fully human. The philanderer may, on occasion, be a colorful type, but my experience is that he forfeits some critical part of his humanity by his faithlessness.

But to come back to the young couples of whom we were speaking, most of whom I know and care for: They are not monsters of depravity or selfishness. They are, for the most part, intelligent, kind, and well-intentioned. They pride themselves on being careful and kindly in their relations with others, respecting other opinions and other ways of life. Why, then, do they do so much damage to each other? Surely not because of wickedness but because of false ideas.

To write the natural history of the odd notions that seem so strongly lodged in their brains would take a volume or two; I have no heart for it in any event. I care for them, and it hurts and angers me to see them wound each other in the name of freedom and openness.

It has been said that the Puritans didn't prevent sin, they just took the fun out of it. I suspect that's impossible or sin wouldn't have remained so popular through the ages. It has, in any event, remained for the modern age to make sin virtually impossible by absorbing it into one popular psychological theory or another.

I can't worry too much about the wives and husbands of my own generation. The greater part of those who are happily married or reasonably so will doubtless remain that way. At least I hope so. Those who are determined to "find themselves" to pursue their lost youth will also do so. They at least know what they are giving up.

It's those of another generation who don't even understand the principle of fidelity that I mourn for. What will the ripeness of years mean to them when the landscapes of their lives are strewn with the wreckage of dead romances?

The Original
| 1953 | Fourth
of July Parade

In the eyes of the public the professional historian is apt to appear rather like a dour and precocious child at a birthday party who, armed with a pin, goes around bursting the other children's brightly colored balloons and making withering remarks about juveniles who play with such baubles. He is always lurking about to deny a Chamber of Commerce contention that George Washington slept here or to refute the story that Betsy Ross made the first Flag.

Each year, as we approach our greatest national holiday, one of our tribe is sure to be overheard muttering that the thirteen Colonies actually became free and independent States through a resolution passed by the Continental Congress on July 2, 1776, and that the Declaration of Independence wasn't signed until August 2. If pressed hard he will admit reluctantly that SOMETHING happened on the 4th of July. Although the Colonies had declared themselves independent two days earlier, Jefferson's Declaration was adopted by Congress on the 4th.

Jefferson's document exalted the principles of human equality and freedom to the level of cherished national ideals. But the Declaration, however eloquent and noble, was simply the statement of an aspiration. All such statements, if they are to endure, must find embodiment in the political and institutional life of a nation. To the Founding Fathers this could only be accomplished through a federal union, indissoluble and perpetual, with carefully defined powers. Liberty, in their view, could only be secured through wise and firm laws that operated equally on all the people, and the great destiny of the country could only be realized if the individual States could be persuaded to surrender a portion of their cherished sovereignty to a strong national government.

At Philadelphia in the muggy summer of 1787, the conservative statesmen of the new republic labored to place the United States under law. Together they fashioned, after much debate, the federal Constitution and then, with no little anxiety, submitted their handiwork for the approval of the people of the States.

The opposition of sincere men who saw the Constitution simply as a stalking horse for "the money interest" was determined and often bitter. In the critical state of Massachusetts it took astute political maneuvering and the prestige of ailing Governor John Hancock to secure ratification by the narrowest of margins.

With the approval of nine states needed to bring the new government into being, it was June 25, 1788, before New Hampshire, the ninth state, joined the ranks of the ratifiers. Five days later Virginia, one of the most important states of all, added her ratification. In the Tidewater State, Patrick Henry, a bitter opponent of the new government, had exhausted all listeners with the effusions of his famed oratory. "What can avail," he had asked his fellow delegates in the Virginia ratifying convention, "your specious imaginary balances, your rope-dancing, cabin-rattling, ridiculous ideal checks and balances?"

At last the weary recording clerk abandoned his efforts to keep pace with the flood of eloquence and simply noted, "Here Mr. Henry strongly and pathetically expatiated on the probability of the President's enslaving America and the horrid consequences that must result."

It had taken the logic of Madison, Washington's moral force, and the popularity of Marshall to counterbalance the eloquence of Virginia's popular hero.

With news of Virginia's ratification the joy of the Federalists was complete. Everywhere that a handful of friends to the new Constitution met bonfires flared and endless toasts were drunk to the federal document, to peace and prosperity, to freedom and the rule of reason, to France, to General Washington, to justice, to law and liberty.

Such demonstrations were all very well, but the triumphant Federalists of Philadelphia felt that it behooved the first true people's republic in the history of the world to express itself with a dignity consonant with the greatness of the moment.

Hardly a week remained before the day suited above all others for a celebration of the ratification. The anniversary of the Declaration of Independence was already a national holiday observed each year with oratory, parades, and fireworks. The 4th of July, 1788, would be a day unique in the history of Pennsylvania, indeed in the history of man. Independence and the new Constitution would be celebrated together, and the two documents would thus be associated with each other in the popular mind—the treasured proclamation of freedom and equality and the new frame of government that had been attacked in some quarters as a treacherous betrayal of the principles of the Revolution.

Plans were made for a "Grand Procession" and the whole city was thrown into a turmoil of activity. Under the relentless eye of the summer sun, carpenters, wheelwrights, cabinetmakers, and ships' joiners worked to prepare for the approaching holiday.

Dawn, July 4, 1788, was greeted by the bells of Christ Church, and the procession, surely the most magnificent in American history, began to form.

At nine o'clock it started to move along the cobbled streets of the city. Leading the marchers was the mounted figure of John Nixon, a prominent merchant of the city, who carried a staff surmounted by the cap of liberty and bearing a silk flag inscribed "July 4, 1776." Behind him came another of the city's panjandrums riding on the horse of General Rochambeau who led the French forces at Yorktown.

Next in line came a carriage built in the form of an eagle and drawn by six white horses. The Chief Justice of the Pennsylvania Supreme Court rode on the eagle's back supporting a pole that bore a framed replica of the new Constitution with the words "the people" below it. The carriage, painted a light blue, was twenty feet long. The eagle, mounted on springs, rose to a height of thirteen feet. On its breast was a shield containing thirteen stars and the claws of the huge bird clutched an olive branch and thirteen arrows.

Behind the eagle, as it swayed over the cobblestones, came ten gentlemen representing the States that had ratified the Constitution. Their arms were locked to symbolize the Union.

Following them came the New Roof, or Federal Edifice, drawn by ten horses. Its dome was supported by thirteen columns, three of which were still incomplete. On top of the dome was a cupola surmounted by Plenty with her overflowing cornucopia. The whole structure was thirty-six feet high and around its pedestal was the motto "In Union the Fabric Stands Firm."

Four hundred and fifty architects and house carpenters marched behind the Federal Edifice. Next in line came the Agricultural Society and then the Manufacturing Society.

The Manufacturing Society had prepared a carriage on which was demonstrated the whole process for manufacturing cloth. Eighty spindles were weaving and attractive girls were busy designing and printing "elegant chintz patterns." Around the float were the words, "May the government protect the manufacturers of America."

The most spectacular feature of the procession was the Federal ship *Union.* Mounting twenty guns and carrying a crew of twenty-five, the thirty-four-foot ship had been built from her keep to her last stay and yard in four days. As the wheeled vessel was drawn through the streets of Philadelphia, her officers gave orders, sails were trimmed, the anchor cast and weighed, and the cannon fired.

Beyond the *Union* marched the sailmakers and boatbuilders and 330 ship carpenters.

Coach painters marched past in clean aprons, carrying pallets and brushes. Then came the cabinetmakers, porters, watchmakers, fringe and ribbon weavers, tailors, coopers, carvers, and gilders, all dressed in the costumes and carrying the implements of their trades.

The line seemed endless: stonecutters, gunsmiths, saddlers, distillers, tobacconists, upholsterers, brewers, tanners. There was even a French corsetmaker and his apprentice, the latter carrying "an elegant pair of lady's stays."

Next came the clergy, including a Jewish rabbi, walking arm in arm, and behind them, probably to preclude bad jokes, came the physicians of the city. Scattered through the marching column were several bands, the city militia, and officials of the city and State.

Followed by the spectators, the procession filed, hot and thirsty, onto the lawn at Bush Hill to hear the oration that was already an established feature of the holiday. A battery of guns, missing their proper cue, fired thirteen volleys during the address but the final words rang out, clear and inspiring, "Liberty, virtue and religion go hand in hand, harmoniously protecting, enlivening and exalting all. Happy country, may thy happiness be perpetual."

At the end of the speech the crowd descended gratefully upon tables laden with a "cold collation," and quenched its thirst with American cider and American beer.

That night the city celebrated with fireworks, and ten ships on the Delaware, representing the ratifying states, were brilliantly illuminated. Even nature cooperated by festooning the night sky with an aurora borealis that must have seemed to patriotic hearts a sign of heavenly approbation.

Thus, on America's greatest 4th of July, the Constitution and the Declaration of Independence, polestars of the American faith, shared a place in the hearts of patriotic Philadelphians as they have done since in the hearts of all Americans. Liberty seemed finally secure under law.

The Founders

and the Court

The recent decisions of the Supreme Court in the so-called civil rights cases have raised a storm of controversy. As with the decision on school integration, those who have found the decisions of the court distasteful charge that it is usurping powers that the framers of the Constitution never intended it to have.

Support for this position can be found in Article III of the Constitution, especially Section 2, which deals with the jurisdiction of the court. In Section 2, nothing is said specifically about the power of the court to pass on the constitutionality of legislative acts.

Certainly some of the delegates to the convention and many of those who opposed ratification of the Constitution by the states feared that the court would come to exercise undue power in the new government. But there was a hard core of delegates (and these were, generally speaking, the members who would properly be considered the principal architects of the Constitution) who fought from the first for a powerful court with the right to review all acts of the legislature.

There is no mistaking the intent of these delegates; they wished to fashion a frame of government with an effective executive and a strong and independent judiciary.

Almost without exception the leading political writers of the eighteenth century agreed that a republican form of government was only practical in small nations. Efforts to extend republics over wide areas had invariably resulted in failure; history demonstrated that monarchy was best suited to administer a vast territory.

The lesson was obvious to most of the American statesmen of the Revolutionary era; a republican form of government had little chance of success in the United States. Yet the delegates to the federal convention were emotionally and intellectually committed to the novel experiment of a republican government for the new nation, which, although it extended over a considerable portion of a vast continent, could never have been brought to accept a monarchial form of government. The conclusion was quite apparent to those who led the fight for a new national government. In a balanced government, the executive and the judiciary represented the monarchial principle. Therefore these must be strengthened as far as a republican system permitted.

James Madison, who, with such allies as Gouverneur Morris, Rufus King, and James Wilson, represented the nationalist group in the convention, prepared the Virginia Plan, which was offered to the delegates when they convened in Philadelphia in May 1787.

The Virginia Plan provided, among other things, for a Council of Revision composed of "the executive and a convenient number of the national judiciary," with "authority to examine every act of the national Legislature before it shall operate and every act of particular legislature [state] before a negative thereon shall be final."

That is to say, before an act passed by Congress could become the law of the land, under the terms of the Virginia Plan, it first had to be approved by the Council of Revision, which would examine it, especially in regard to its constitutionality.

The national judiciary itself was given appellate jurisdiction in maritime cases, "cases in which foreigners or citizens of other states . . . may be interested, impeachments of national officers and questions which may involve the national peace and harmony."

In defending the Council of Revision, James Wilson pointed out that "laws may be unjust, may be unwise, may be dangerous, may be destructive, and yet not be so unconstitutional as to justify the judges (of the Supreme Court) in refusing to give them effect." A Council of Revision would nip such laws in the bud.

There had been no suggestion at this date, it might be said parenthetically, that a bill of rights be added to the Constitution, and Wilson and his allies were concerned that Congress might pass laws which, while not technically in violation of the Constitution, were nonetheless against "natural law and equity"—in other words, which infringed rights of the individual that had been won in centuries of struggle against the arbitrary powers of the Crown.

The advocates of the Council of Revision had, in the final version of the Constitution, to accept a Supreme Court with less extensive powers than they would have wished, but a court which might nonetheless, by slow and gradual accretion of power, come eventually to play the role that the nationalists had from the first envisioned for it.

And so it turned out. James Wilson and John Blair, both delegates to the Federal Convention, were on the first court, and from their earliest decisions the majority of the justices showed that they had no doubts about the right of the court to exercise powers, among them the right to declare acts of Congress unconstitutional, that were not among those enumerated in the Constitution.

When Congress in 1792 passed the Invalid Pensions Act, requiring the justices of the courts on circuit to hear the pension claims of Revolutionary veterans, the justices did not hesitate to denounce the law as unconstitutional.

The response of Congress was prompt and predictable. Indignant legislators demanded that the judges be impeached for contesting the supremacy of Congress. The Constitution, they argued, granted no such rights to the Supreme Court.

The justices, keeping their own council, weathered the storm and continued to give notice at every opportunity that they conceived of their jurisdiction as extending over a far wider range of cases than might be indicated by a strict interpretation of Article III. The Federalists, as proponents of a strong national government, supported and applauded the court's growing power, while the Jeffersonians viewed the process with noisy apprehension.

If the federal Constitution is more than the bare words of the text itself, it is all that history has endowed it with. The effort, however brief and partial, to say what the Constitution is must take account of what its framers intended it to be, but even more of what it in fact became by the interplay between the intentions of those charged with administering it and the pressures created by a vital and expanding society.

Few historians doubt that the principal framers of our government intended that the executive and judicial branches should exercise a check on the legislative. This much the record shows.

The record shows also that, in the early years of the new government, the men charged with giving effect to the often skimpy blueprint sketched out in the Constitutional Convention labored to the same end. Whether this end was a proper one is, of course, another matter.

Since the argument from authority is not necessarily authoritative, the fact that most of the Founding Fathers believed in the necessity of a strong executive and of a national judiciary with the right to review the acts of Congress does not make those propositions right. That is another question and one to which indeed it may be impossible to give an objective answer.

Ford's
1974 Pardon
of Nixon

Two weeks after the pardon of Richard Nixon, I seem to be alone among my friends—whether liberal or conservative—in applauding President Ford's action. Thus, I feel it necessary to state my reasons as explicitly as possible. First I will list a common objection to the pardon and then my rebuttal, adding some moral or philosophical reflections:

Objection: The pardon will prevent the whole truth about Watergate from being revealed.

Rebuttal: The essential truth is already known. Only details remain to be discovered. The evidence of corruption and abuse of power is so overwhelming that some forty people have been indicted, convicted, or have served or are presently serving jail sentences. The President of the United States has been deposed. To keep piling up new evidence of wrongdoing would be the greatest example of legal overkill in our history.

Objection: The trials of John Mitchell, H. R. Haldeman, and John Ehrlichman, three of the most culpable members of the Watergate conspiracy, will be aborted by the Nixon pardon.

Rebuttal: This is clearly not the case. The fact that Nixon cannot now refuse to testify at their trials on the grounds of self-incrimination may even aid the prosecution and bring out new facts regarding the conspiracy.

Objection: When Nixon can get away with crimes for which an ordinary citizen would go to jail, there is no real "equality before the law" in America.

Rebuttal: Of course, there is no "equal justice." We all recognize that the powerful or prominent individual who breaks the law almost invariably suffers less severe legal penalties than, say, a hippie or a poor black. Pardoning Nixon merely proves what we already know.

This fact is insufficient reason, however, for not continually struggling to achieve "equal justice" in the United States. Beyond this, far from "getting away with" criminal acts, Nixon, with his inordinate lust for power and his obsession with the acclaim of posterity, has suffered greater humiliation than any other major political figure in our history. His fall from the most powerful office in the world is more personally punishing than any of the penalties that the law provides. The doctrine and practice of "equal justice" will not, in the long run, be compromised by the pardon.

Beyond these specific, practical points lie some of deeper significance. Down through history, whenever an individual—king, prime minister, tyrant, or ruler of whatever sort—has been deposed, his subjects, however much they may have previously professed to love, admire, or merely respect him, have customarily turned on him with vindictive fury and sought to degrade and, finally, physically destroy him.

There is, I believe, something in our collective psyche that needs and yearns for power and authority. This yearning puffs up the possessors of such power until they are mythical projections of our own subconscious needs, rather than perceived as real human beings. Transformed into demigods, they can do no wrong.

When they fall, their subjects, people, or constituents turn on them with a bitter sense of betrayal. They wish to punish the fallen leader for the collapse of their own illusions. That is when the ambiguity of their feelings for the leader is revealed. Even as they loved and acclaimed the leader (or his power), they also subconsciously feared and resented him.

This can be translated, if you wish, into Freudian terms. Once the leader has fallen, we would immolate—annihilate—him, because his fall is perceived as a betrayal. Never before, of course, had Americans experienced this classic historical event; indeed, we had imagined it could never happen in a more or less democratic country. But, clearly, it can and has.

This reaction, in my opinion, underlies the hue and cry over the Nixon pardon. I believe it explains the continuing vindictiveness that the majority of Americans feel toward a ruined and defeated man.

On the other hand, the minority of us who support the pardon find its ultimate justification in mercy, a blessed virtue. Perceiving ourselves as a humane people (at least nominally), we applaud Mr. Ford's wise and compassionate act. He has spared the country, the Presidency, and justice itself from a difficult burden—the interminable months that would have been required to complete judicial proceedings against an ailing and pitiable figure.

Earlier I published an article comparing impeachment to regicide— killing the king. We have now endured the trauma of that symbolic act: Nixon, as king-president, was, for all practical purposes, impeached— symbolically slain. Surely that should be punishment enough.

Civilization:
1975 It's the Little
Things That Count

As an assiduous student of the rise and fall of civilizations, I am aware that it is often the apparently insignificant things that matter most.

Some historians suggest that the decline of Rome was directly related to the introduction of a marvelous new system of plumbing in which water was carried throughout the city by lead pipes. Those who take this line point out that a substantial number of Romans who could afford this technological breakthrough died of lead poisoning. Since these included a large proportion of the intellectual and political elite of the empire, decay and disintegration were the inevitable results of their untimely demises.

Closer to home, Lynn White, the distinguished medievalist of UCLA, has argued that the invention of the stirrup (or its adoption) made possible the military tactics of mounted shock combat—the knight with his lance—and hence the rise of feudalism.

It might, therefore, be said to follow that no stone is too small to leave unturned in the historian's eternal search for the cause or causes of the decline and fall of great powers.

Fifty years ago Oswald Spengler wrote a startling book called *Decline of the West*, in which he maintained that the West, like Rome and Nineveh before it, was in the early stages of an irreversible decline. For a time the remarkable prosperity of the Western world seemed to give lie to his thesis.

Now we are not so sure. Many of those manners and mores traditionally identified with the decline and fall of civilizations can be observed in present-day society: sexual license (or perhaps, more accurately, rampant sexuality), violence, crime, overcrowding of cities and underpopulation of the countryside, loss of religious faith, rising rates of suicide, alcoholism, drug addiction, divorce, and abortion (characteristic of the decadent period of the Roman Empire), the proliferation of mystery cults, the growth of the military state, the centralization of power, the rise of the obtuse bureaucrat, and, above all, inflation, the most insidious destroyer of civilizations.

There are, in my view, many hopeful signs of new stirrings and new energies, so the picture is not one of unrelieved gloom.

Be all that as it may, as a historian my task is, at least theoretically, to seek out the causes of the decline we appear to be in. And to do this I have concentrated my attention on the so-far-unnoticed trivia of history.

Since the beginnings of human society, man and woman have slept on the floor or the ground. Most of the peoples of the earth still do. It was Western man and woman who in their vanity and presumption or desire for luxuriousness and dissipation raised the bed off the floor. This is probably the beginning of that tension and anxiety which have long been recognized as part of our temperament. It may well be that all crippling neuroses stem from the primitive fear of falling out of bed in the middle of some bad dream (caused by sleeping above the floor) or in the midst of some romantic dalliance.

Having identified this, the basic cause of our decline, I have traced several important subsidiary causes. One that may appear trifling to the uninitiated is the belt. Yes, I mean that strange device that modern Western man, as distinguished from almost every other man in every other culture, wraps and buckles around his middle. Certainly, it is true that men have been "girding up their loins" at least since biblical times. But they have done it as a prelude to battle; no ancient man would have dreamed of going about with his guts all cinched in and his intestines constricted.

In modern times, rational individuals among us have preferred suspenders, proving that not everyone need succumb to the tyranny of fashion. The superiority of the suspender to the belt is so plain, lucid, clear, and inescapable that we must, in fact, look beyond mere fashion for the strange ubiquity of the belt.

We must call on that arcane science, psychology, for assistance. And psychology obligingly yields the answer: the belt is, in its most basic essential essence, a symbolic separation of the loins from the brain. It represents in specific, material form that division between the rational and the irrational, between the id and the ego in Freudian terms, that we now understand to be one of the wounds of modern "civilized" Western man. In addition, it is damn uncomfortable. And unhealthy. American males, who are the premier belt-wearers of the world, have the worst stomachs in the world—this is not, to be sure, simply due to belts, but belts are a major part of the problem.

The other part is due to modern refrigeration, which allows us to constantly pour cold liquids into our highly sensitive centers.

Cold drinks, the colder the better, are one of the triumphs of modern technology. Binding up our guts with constricting belts and then flushing them continually with cold drinks—that is a recipe for calamity if there ever was one. No wonder Americans consume more antacid stomach-settling potions than all the rest of mankind. The American stomach is, quite simply, one of the disaster areas of the world.

So, having produced our primal anxiety by sleeping above the floor, we compounded the error by wearing belts, thereby symbolically severing the genitals from the brain and helping to ruin the stomach in the process.

Not satisfied with two egregious errors, we added a third—the indoor flush toilet. The vast majority of mankind for the greater portion of human history has existed without the benefit of indoor plumbing. This was for two reasons: the technology for such a marvel did not exist—or water was too scarce—and human waste was a resource that could not be cast aside in most of the agricultural economies of the world.

The indoor-flush-toilet fallacy was brought home to me quite vividly not long ago when we used a friend's fishing cabin with an outdoor john. It was out of the house, an outhouse. That was the point. You had to go out of the house.

I am not going to elaborate on the pleasures of the outhouse, present and past, although it takes a degree of restraint on my part not to. But I am going to point out that one of the diagnoses of the malaise of modern man attributes the attrition of our effective life to our divorce from nature. No man or woman who frequented an outhouse could be very far from nature or fail to experience it in all its vagaries.

So there it is. The decline of the West (with particular emphasis on the decline of our portion of North America) is not due to the energy crisis, to Watergate, to the military-industrial complex, or to Vietnam. Those are all only symptoms of a far more deeply seated illness, a malady of the spirit that began when we ascended to raised beds, was accentuated by belts and cold drinks, and was compounded by the indoor flush toilet.

What this suggests to me is that all is not lost; a decline such as this can, after all, be reversed. It is simple enough to start sleeping on the floor once more—many young people already do. And begin wearing suspenders rather than belts (I do).

Outhouses pose more of a problem, especially in cities. But this is a problem worth tackling. In my own community, the newspaper devotes more space each week to how to dispose of sewage than to any other subject. And no other issue arouses more passionate feeling. (History, which abounds in ironies, offers few as engaging as the preoccupation of the most advanced civilization in the world with the disposal of its own waste.)

So that is it: We must get back to the basics—and once we have, we may see the end of our decline. You see, it *is* the little things that count.

Decisions,

Decisions!
They're Driving Us Daft

The condition of modern man has been described as that of being nib-
bled to death by mice. It is my contention that our psychic energies are
daily eroded by what I would call pseudodecisions.

These are decisions that the vast majority of us are called on to make
every day between unimportant or meaningless alternatives. I further
believe that this wearisome multiplicity of decisions is a manifestation
of a late or decadent phase of what might be called industrial-technological capitalism, one of whose principal accomplishments has been
the much-acclaimed "free market."

The origin of the free market—laissez-faire—can be found in the
ideas of Adam Smith and his disciples in the late eighteenth and nineteenth centuries. In its simplest form, the notion of the free market derived from the doctrine that the general good was best served by leaving
aggressive and ambitious entrepreneurs—a fancy term for businessmen—free to pursue their own interests.

Extraordinarily flexible and efficient, the free market system found
one potent expression in the great mail-order catalogues of the nineteenth century, recently reprinted as an exercise in nostalgia. The catalogues are, of course, much more than that. They represent one of the
supreme achievements of democratic capitalism. In their interminable
pages one could be confident of finding a better and cheaper incubator,
rattrap, carriage, or corset.

But the free market, it is now clear, became intoxicated with its own
facility. From producing a remarkable variety of practical and inexpen-

sive "things," it went on to produce a vast array of other "things" that nobody needed but that, it turned out, they could be persuaded, if bombarded by ingenious advertisers, to believe they needed.

Not only could the free market produce an infinite variety of things less and less needed, but within each species of thing, so to speak, it could produce another whole level of varieties. Thus, there were not only a number of cars by different automobile makers to choose from but each automobile maker had, in turn, a wide range of models involving the most subtle differences—differences often without a distinction. Inexpensiveness and efficiency were the principal victims of variety.

For example, the Model-T Ford was, like the Montgomery Ward catalogue, one of the high spots of modern capitalism. Its price and efficiency were the wonder of the world. In large part, this was because, for all practical purposes, there was only one model—the Model-T.

Nevertheless, the temptation to variety and multiplicity proved irresistible. This was the heresy of industrial-technological capitalism: to make variety into the highest good—a variety that contributes little or nothing to human welfare, happiness, or even comfort but that, on the contrary, is enormously costly in economic and psychological terms.

That, above all, is the point I wish to emphasize. The human and material resources that go into creating twenty-eight models where one or two would do very well (or indeed much better) is a heavy charge against our energy reserves (not to mention, of course, the "energy"—time and money—devoted to persuading the public that one dog food or deodorant is substantially better than another).

These are obvious "costs," generally recognized and widely commented on. Less frequently noted are the time and energy expended in choosing between all the tantalizing but essentially meaningless alternatives:

Which model?
Which flavor?
Which position?
Which color?
The average American may be imagined to live a day like this.

Which cereal for breakfast: Hotsy Totsy, Special F, New K Flakes, Nuts
& Pops (sugar or honey-coated), Bangs, Crumbles, Zips? Then what to
eat at lunch, again out of a bewildering variety of dishes?

For a casual afternoon ice cream cone—what flavor? Cherry Bur-
gundy Muscatel or Peanut Butter and Jelly? Or Bubblegum?

Then, after a day of energy-draining decisions, large and small, the
average American returns home to a baffling choice of interchangeable
TV programs, and finally, most distracting of all, he must decide what
position to assume in love making. Wearily, he takes up the sex manual.
Position 12? Tried that last week. Position 23? Too exhausting after a
day of decision making. The wife wants to try 47, he prefers 19. They
compromise on 33.

Unsuccessfully.

I doubt if humanity suffered when there were only two standard flavors of ice cream—chocolate and vanilla, with fresh peach or straw-
berry in season. For one thing, it was genuine ice cream, not synthetic
goop. Or half a dozen makes of car with two or three models of each. Or
restaurants that offered a choice of two or three meals, nonfrozen and
skillfully prepared. And two or three positions, or even one, for sexual
intercourse.

My concern is not so much with variety as with luxury, or even with
its exorbitant material cost for such shallow and meretricious rewards;
it is with the psychic or human cost—in time, in energy, in attention.

Decisions! Decisions! That is the baffled cry of modern man. Nib-
bled to death by mice, eroded by pseudodecisions, he has little nerve or
resolution for the more serious decisions that confront individuals and
societies. This may be the real measure of our decadence.

It is not that there is anything immoral in thirty-one flavors, twenty-
eight models, and sixty-four positions. It is simply that they assist us in
wasting the ultimate human resource, time (or energy). Of that, it
seems to me, we already have far too little.

The New
[1982] Abolitionism

The notion of human slavery, of owning human beings as property, of beating or mutilating them as punishment, of selling children away from their mothers and wives from their husbands, is an idea so repugnant to the modern consciousness that it is hard to comprehend the fact that such practices were commonplace in the United States a little more than a hundred years ago. When we think of such matters they seem infinitely remote, as though they had happened ages past. Such an institution could never have survived into the present age, we assure ourselves. If the Civil War had not plucked up slavery, an enlightened nation would, by the opening decades of the twentieth century, have renounced it as incompatible with everything that America stands for. "Progress," in its inevitable march, would have made slavery an anachronism. Industrialization would have made it uneconomic.

The facts are otherwise. From the beginning of the Republic, the institution of slavery put down deeper and deeper roots, becoming increasingly brutal and repressive with each passing decade. Far from deploring the institution, Southerners began to glorify it, comparing the culture it had produced in the South to that of ancient Greece, another slave-holding society. It was the settled determination of the South to extend the protection of the federal government to slaves as property westward to the Pacific Ocean and northward as far as Canada. Indeed, they wished to add Cuba to the slave empire.

"Progress," however we define that often ambiguous word, has demonstrated no built-in capacity for regenerating the moral fibre of a people. It has, if anything, displayed a disconcerting capacity to come to terms with exploitation and repression in the name of progress.

How then were the slaves freed? Quite simply, by the heroic efforts of individuals who dedicated their lives to the antislavery cause. They took the name abolitionists. Moral gadflies, tireless agitators, proclaimers of a moral order in the universe, champions of Christian brotherhood, they pricked the conscience of their fellow citizens. They allowed them no rest on the issue of slavery. Day in and day out, year in and year out, relentless and indefatigable, they pressed the issue. Mobbed, beaten, denounced, shut out from the company of respectable people, they persisted. They grew from a handful into an army. When Richard Henry Dana undertook to defend runaway slaves in Boston, friends of a lifetime cut him dead on the streets.

The great mass of Americans north of Mason's and Dixon's Line were quite ready to concede the iniquity of slavery, but they simply wished to forget about the whole subject. They didn't want trouble; they didn't like agitators. Agitators were bad for business. Northerners had other things on their minds like making a living or "dropping out" West, or quarreling over "hard" money versus "soft" money. Their relative indifference to the moral dimensions of the slavery issue demonstrated the ability of a people to ignore or suppress crucial moral issues. In this respect Americans were no different from the vast majority of species. We are all disposed to accept things-as-they-are as having a kind of inevitability about them. They seem part of the landscape, part of the complex set of ideas that define the society as a whole. Dangerous things to tamper with.

We find ourselves today in much the same situation that our forefathers did in the era before the Civil War (which of course was not fought primarily to free the slaves). We have allowed an evil, a horror of almost incomprehensible proportions, to grow up in our midst and come indeed to seem like part of the natural order of things, as inevitable as the sunrise in the morning or the passage of the seasons. We have knowingly and deliberately armed ourselves with the most terrible weapons of destruction conceivable. As people originally dedicated to "emancipating" the world, we have devised and built weapons capable of destroying it many times over. Most astonishing of all (and, one might add, most obscene), we have done this in the name of peace. We have solemnly declared a moral enormity of staggering proportions to be our regretted but necessary duty.

To inform the world that we may have to destroy the greater part of it in order to save it from communism (or anything else) is an arrogant presumption which, so far as I know, is without precedent in history. (Perhaps the will has been there before but never the capacity.) Indeed, having stated it, one stares at it unbelievingly on the page. Clearly what is involved in part is a dangerously diminished moral sensibility, but perhaps even more important, a badly flawed notion of the meaning of human existence. The world, believe me, was not created (or has not evolved) to be the creature of the United States, to be shaped or destroyed, in accordance with our Will, reinforced by stockpiles of atomic weapons.

Peoples throughout history have lived and suffered under governments far more egregiously tyrannical than any communist regime presently existing in the world. At least they or their children survived to see better times. Now the United States declares that it is prepared, if it deems it necessary to do so, to foreclose a future for the human race by employing nuclear weapons against its communist adversary. Assuming the worst scenario—an impending communist global takeover—I suspect that the peoples of the world might prefer, for a time at least, to live under communist regimes rather than not to live at all, to have no successors that could be called human. Or at the very least to have a say in the matter.

Perhaps the crowning irony is that at the same time that we are preparing to destroy millions upon millions of Russians because they live under a system called communism, we announce that the system itself is collapsing, to quote Karl Marx, from its internal inconsistencies (as every "system" must in time). Moreover, there seems to be some evidence to support the assertion.

I do not covet the mantle of prophecy (I have my hands full with the past) but I see no conceivable reasons to believe that the human race will follow undeviatingly either the path of Russian Communism or American Capitalism (indeed the best thing that can be said of the latter is that it has avoided the worst excesses of the former). Surely the future, if we allow it to happen, must hold something better than either.

Which brings us back to the abolitionists. There is only one overriding issue facing the United States and the world, a single issue beside which *all* other issues fade to relative insignificance, and that is the complete outlawing and destruction of all nuclear weapons and weapons systems, beginning in the United States. We must begin in the United States, because the United States is still a democracy, if a highly imperfect one, and the citizens of this nation can still make their convictions felt through their elected representatives.

If the day comes when 75 percent of all Americans (or even, perhaps, 55 percent) announce with clarity and conviction, "We will not tolerate the existence of a nuclear arsenal in a nation that once called itself Christian and professed to be dedicated to improving the condition of all peoples, everywhere," that nuclear arsenal will be dismantled and mankind will breathe more freely. To bring the people of this Republic to such a conviction will not be quickly or easily accomplished. It may take as long as it took the abolitionists to free the slaves and as much heroism and devotion, as much willingness to endure hostility and abuse, charges of being unpatriotic or of being a "commie lover" (as the abolitionists were accused of being "nigger lovers" and proudly confessed to being).

I, for one, am willing to confess myself as a "commie lover," because my faith so instructs me. Indeed, I love the commies more than the capitalists—though I deplore the system under which they live—because I suspect they are substantially more in need of love. Certainly, the thought of destroying millions or dozens or *one of them* because they give their allegiance to a different political system than I do fills me with repugnance and dismay (not to mention, of course, the millions upon millions of those who will, it seems clear, be quite coincidentally annihilated).

IN THE NAME OF GOD, LET US ABOLISH NUCLEAR WEAPONS.

Our leaders tell us that such talk is defeatist, un-American. It is true I have no nerve or will for these murderous games, these scenarios of destruction with their insane calculations of kills and overkills. Nations as well as individuals can go insane. It seems clear to me that the United States is at this moment collectively insane in its policies and attitudes toward the Soviet Union. I know of no other way to explain our continuing accumulation of the deadliest weapons.

Slavery was such a madness; the cure was slow and ultimately terrible, but we must never for a moment lose sight of the fact that it was accomplished finally by the conscious, intelligent, sacrificial efforts of a host of individuals not strikingly different from ourselves. A group of pacifist organizations have joined forces recently to distribute "The New Abolitionist Covenant." It is most appropriately named. Only a modern abolitionist covenant to do away with nuclear arms, utterly and completely, can save mankind from something very like destruction and the United States from bearing the primary guilt for the holocaust (though most of us presumably will be dead in any event).

Samuel Eliot
| 1976 | Morison, 1887–1976

I first encountered Samuel Eliot Morison—the Grand Old Man of American historians who died recently in Boston at age eighty-eight— when I was a graduate student in history at Harvard. The year was 1947.

One day at the end of class I was summoned, almost imperiously, for tea at the elegant Morison home on Brimmer Street. Although he never told me the reason for the invitation, I subsequently deduced that the honor had been bestowed because he liked the paper I had written on Samuel Adams.

After that visit, intrigued by Morison's own work in colonial history as well as by his style of writing, I decided to specialize—every graduate student had to specialize—in early American history.

Morison specialized within his specialty, becoming a historian of early seafarers to America. A prolific author, writing in the narrative style, as opposed to the merely analytical, Morison published his first book in 1913 and his last, the second volume of his *European Discovery of America*, more than six decades later. In between he wrote, among other books, the fifteen-volume *History of U.S. Naval Operations in World War II* (while he was a reserve officer) and the *Oxford History of the American People* and collaborated with Henry Steele Commager on the classic college textbook, the *Growth of the American Republic*.

While pursuing my Ph.D., I became Morison's graduate assistant or reader, grading papers and performing other academic chores. By the time my wife and I left Harvard four or five years later, we had often been guests at the Brimmer Street house, had sailed with Morison on his yawl, the *Emily Marshall*, and had come, indeed, to feel almost like members of the family.

When my younger son, Eliot, was born, Morison consented to be his godfather. He assisted me in getting my first teaching job at UCLA (he had begun his teaching career at Berkeley)—although he warned me that California was where historians past their prime were turned out to graze. He suspected that in such a seductive atmosphere I would be tempted to spend my time lolling in the sun rather than pursuing those vigorous scholarly tasks required to win promotion within the University of California. I was so impressed by this rather grim forecast that for my first few years in lotus land I hardly dared step out of the house.

Boston and California are a continent (perhaps a century) apart. We saw Morison and his new wife, Priscilla, infrequently, although they came to the new campus of UC-Santa Cruz for the dedication of a student residence hall named after him (not by me, I must note, but by the students). There he gave a marvelous lecture on Admiral Perry, whose biography he had just finished, and participated benignly in the dedication of Morison House.

One incident stands out in my recollection of the visit. When the Morisons were touring the college, a Panlike student with then-uncommon beard and long hair, upon being introduced to Priscilla Morison, extracted a flower from his beard and presented it to her with a courtly air. To which she replied, in something between an exclamation and a plea, "Mercy!"

Even then, in 1967, Mrs. Morison, many years younger than her husband, was fighting cancer. She died of it six years later, and he began his last great labor of love, an adoring biography of her published privately last year.

After her death, hearing that he was infirm, I traveled to his summer home, Good Hope, on Maine's Mt. Desert Island. I was well aware, as he was, that it might be my last visit. The better part of two days that we spent together in late summer, 1974, were profoundly instructive to me in the grandeur and courage of at least his old age. Everywhere he pointed out reminders of his beloved wife: the house they had planned together, the garden she had helped design, the shrubs and flowers she had planted. Her spirit presided still.

Morison's legs were failing him. He walked with great difficulty. But he swam freely and exuberantly in the pool that he had built with the money from one of his many awards. Concealed by a grove of trees, one ancient historian and one middle-aged one skinny-dipped in the declining days of summer.

Sunday morning he made his way with infinite pain and the aid of a walking stick along a rocky ledge, down a long ramp to a float where a small skiff was tied. Slowly, so slowly, he lowered himself into the boat while I watched, not daring to presume to help. Then he took up the oars and rowed across the little bay with all the vigor of a young man. The same laborious routine was followed leaving the skiff. We walked several blocks to the little stone Episcopal church and after the service returned as we had come to be taken by neighbors to a nearby island for lunch.

That night he cooked a delicious dinner of mussels and lobster and we talked of the world, his family and mine, of Harvard then and now, of the history of Mt. Desert, which he dearly loved, and of history in general; history as it had happened and history as historians attempted to recount it. Some of the time we sat silently—the admiral was seldom inclined to small talk.

A tidy fire glowed in the living room, and I thought of a vagrant line of poetry from John Masefield on old age: "I cannot wander, / Your cornland, nor your hill-land nor your valleys, / Ever again. . . . Only stay quiet while my mind remembers / The beauty of fire from the beauty of embers."

While Morison could not wander in his old age, he was certainly not "quiet." He remained fully engaged by life and clearly pushed himself every day to the limits of his diminishing physical resources so that one's sense of his infirmity was counterpointed by a vivid impression of an unquenchable vital energy. That, I believe, was why he was such a great historian. He was deeply and constantly involved in the world around him, right to the end.

The next morning it was time to depart. He walked me down the long drive with gentle, old-fashioned courtesy. When I said my inadequate good-bye, he smiled his (to me) always faintly enigmatic smile, and gave a little wave of his hand. Then he turned back to Good Hope.

In Memoriam:
Alan Chadwick,
1909–1980

Dylan Thomas wrote to his father:

Do not go gentle into that good night.
Rage, rage against the dying of the light.

Alan Chadwick went gently into that good night at Green Gulch, surrounded by people who loved and cared for him in a beautiful setting where he had created one of his great gardens. The "dying of the light" that Alan raged against was the light of our twentieth-century civilization, so heedless of the rich bounty of the earth. More than an inspired horticulturist, Alan was like some furious Old Testament prophet, warning of the wages of our sinful treatment of the land. A visionary, he looked at a barren plot of ground and saw it bloom; the herbaceous border would go just there, opening to an enchanting view of the mountains or the ocean. The herb garden, the garden's soul, would be here, in inviting terraces. The arbor would be over there. And magically, and by incredible labors, they appeared in time, or at least the anticipations of them—at Santa Cruz, in Saratoga, at Green Gulch, Covelo, New Market, wherever he paused in his flight from the unendurable realities of our technological society or simply the obtuseness of humankind.

Every garden contained a penance, concrete-like hardpan, often the result of ceaseless tractor tracks, which had to be broken up so that the soil could breathe. This nourished that. That looked like a weed but drew necessary nutrients up from the deeper levels of the ground. Something rested in the shade of something else and in turn encouraged another flower or vegetable. It was all a marvelously intricate world of interdependent growing things, nature lovingly domesticated.

In an age of "collective leadership" Alan Chadwick was as imperious as a King. In a day of carefully modulated tempers and self-conscious "interpersonal relations," he stormed and raged not just at abstractions like laziness or indifference or inattention but at the poor frail flesh of those who were the destined instruments of his terrible, unflinching will. And then suddenly, the consummate actor for whom all the world was a stage, he would be as sunny, as playful, as irresistible as the prince of a fairy tale. An exotic past lay dimly behind him—British naval officer, Shakespearean actor. Pale water colors, the remnants of Puddleston china and silver brought out for state occasions were reassuring evidence that he had not, after all, come from outer space as one was sometimes inclined to suspect.

Everything about him was remarkable and distinctive. His physique, his height and angularity, his face, his hair, his walk. Those who fell under his spell had generally to put up with a good deal. That so many were willing to do so is the best possible testimony to the power of what he had to teach, which was inseparable from the way he taught it and the person he was. Mystic, seer, creator, lover of fine wines and coffees, of caviar and champagne, man of prodigious fury, his life taught us that "nothing great is accomplished without passion." We will find his spirit in the gardens he or his disciples built, exhorting us to do better, to care more, to work harder, to recklessly expend love on an intractable world, to make the world a garden. And in his vision of gardens never built but only dreamed of.

The William James
Association
Newsletter

When I left the University of California at Santa Cruz in 1973, Paul Lee and I started the William James Association, a nonprofit corporation dedicated to good works. For a time we published a newsletter to inform our members of our philosophy and intentions. The pieces that follow are from those newsletters.

These essays will undertake to define various problems in American society to be tackled by the Association. What is at issue, basically, is nothing less than the reconstruction of American society along lines of specific historical imperatives. These imperatives are just that, not random choices, personal preferences, hasty expedients. They are imperatives—things that must be done. There is widespread agreement that many things are wrong in the United States today. More impressive, there is even a broad kind of consensus on what those things are (and they are very fundamental things): the nature of work; the quality of life—in cities, dangerous and exhausting, in the suburbs, affluent and boring, in the towns, constricting and arid; a shocking maldistribution of income (20 percent of the people own 77 percent of the personal wealth in America, over three times that held by the bottom 80 percent); the problems of racist discrimination, a spiritual curse on all those who suffer from it; the degeneration of virtually all large institutions; the abuse of the land—one could go on and on.

It is largely a matter of where one wishes to concentrate and apply a critical analysis. Our preferred point of attack is against all large-scale institutional structures in our society, for reasons we will explain.

The major divisions of opinion occur over what should be done to regenerate the nation. The usual way in which liberals think about this matter involves vast and enormously expensive federal programs for job training and urban renewal. On the other hand, the radical talks about revolution, but it seems clear that he has even less of a notion of how this revolution is to come about than the liberal has a notion of the ability of government bureaucracy to solve our ills. The conservative, for his part, believes that we simply need to recapture the old American values of thrift and hard work.

We believe the only hope for the future of the country lies in the emergence of new attitudes and a new kind of consciousness. At present it is a commonplace to say that there are two cultures: the dominant culture of success and competition, of productivity and affluence, of vast corporate power and interlocking bureaucratic structures at every level, and the subculture, defined largely by its rejection of the dominant culture. This is the romantic "love-the-land" culture of dropouts, dopers, communards, and itinerants, largely middle-class young people who have abjured the American success ethic and chosen lives of voluntary poverty in association with an ethic of disaffiliation. What is so increasingly clear is that our society cannot provide jobs for young people who wish to work and whose job requirements are quite modest in terms of salary expectations. Not wishing to make money, they want interesting and useful tasks to perform.

It thus follows that whatever may be the practical consequences and future history of communes, we must take with the greatest seriousness the message that the extraordinary popularity of the commune movement conveys to us. We understand this message to be, unmistakably, that the hunger for community in the United States is one of our most profound needs, a need that *must* be satisfied in some form or another.

Rosenstock-Huessy has written: "Service in youth, spontaneous service, without the orders of any visible authority, has been the privilege of volunteers, in any period of history. These volunteers have always made history, and rightly so. . . . The volunteers are the ones that heed the new voice first, the new authority, long before it is in the telephone book. They receive it into their systems by a voluntary response to an emergency, to a social scandal, a social evil that they know must be conquered. And nothing that has not been started by volunteers enters the halls of human history. . . . Modern society must put its economy on a mature footing to the extent that the young become an asset as volunteers, instead of a liability as job-hunters."

What is involved in all these issues is the fact that slavery is an inevitable and inescapable aspect of human existence and all man's dreams of a society without slavery, that is to say without menial and degrading work, have been just that—dreams. The advent of modern machines fostered the illusion that mankind could be freed at last from servile labor, but it turned out that instead, men became enslaved to machines and this was in some ways the most demoralizing slavery of all. . . . It was James's great insight that servile, degrading, slavish work had to be done in every society. It was the condition—the permanently hard and sour foundation—of man's higher life. James wanted that work shared, done by successive generations of young people, so that no class or caste would have to do it for a lifetime.

Young men and women, James wrote in 1910, should be dispatched "to coal and iron mines, to freight trains, to fishing fleets in December, to dishwashing, clothes-washing, window-washing, to road-building and tunnel-making, to foundries and stoke-holes, and to the frames of skyscrapers." They would thus take their turns at the most arduous and menial tasks required to sustain our common life.

If it is true (and history, past and present, certainly points in that direction) that slavish labor is part of the human condition, there would seem to be only three alternatives:

(1) A single servile class, caste, or race, must do such work; and this has been the common (one is tempted to say universal) solution in "civilized societies." The exceptions are only to be found in tribal life, though even tribes often make other tribes subsidiary. Or,

(2) Every member of a society, rich or poor, must take his or her turn in performing such slavish tasks. Or,

(3) Each member of a society must do continuously his or her proper portion of the slavish tasks. For modern man only alternatives two or three or a combination of the two are, one hopes, conceivable.

Put another way, society can only be redeemed by everyone doing a number of unpleasant tasks. In fact, only by the sharing of such tasks can the immemorial curse on them be removed or alleviated. This, of course, is true whether the society be socialist, communist, or capitalist. The solution of our capitalist society has been to use certain ethnic minorities (and women) to perform these servile and degrading tasks, by keeping them in a state of social and economic (though not legal) slavery. For laborious and servile work, where "slavery" has been impossible we have undertaken to pay those who perform such tasks more and more money to do them. Thus garbage collectors in large cities hold the cities themselves hostage for larger salaries and better working conditions. An entire metropolitan area can be held up as though at gun point because of its dependence on transportation workers—a growing legion of those who in our huge urban complexes perform what we conceive to be unpleasant but indispensable services. If our society continues on its present course, this number will grow larger (and more demanding) with every passing decade. The eventual result can only be increasing bitterness on the part of a population that becomes at once exploiters and exploited. Thus the transportation worker whose strike prevents a policeman or teacher from getting to work is as much an exploiter as the policeman whose strike exploits the transportation worker by exposing him to being mugged on the subway or on his bus. The final outcome, whether it comes sooner or later, can only be a complete breakdown of urban life.

It is doubtful, moreover, whether the problem of slavery can be solved on the level of government planning, and federal legislation, even if a national consensus could be created on the issue. Such a solution would mean piling bureaucracies on bureaucracies and thus perpetuating the very evils one wishes to eradicate.

The reference point, of course, is the individual. Whether one chooses the Freudian id or original sin or the territorial imperative, there seems to be ground for believing that people have destructive impulses that constantly threaten social comity and order. An analogue on the social and economic level to the negative elements of the human personality is this same slavish work about which we have been talking. In Rosenstock-Huessy's words, "No man is good. But the word or act that links men may be good. And by link-work evil has to be constantly combatted." People cannot be normally and fruitfully linked by word alone; the act must accompany it. Liberal and radical tracts are empty verbiage unless they are accompanied by *acts*, "link-acts" that consciously set out to overcome our individual selfish isolation—our individualism. We could do worse than heed that very traditional Christian maxim of Chairman Mao, "Forget self; serve the people."

All of which brings us back to our basic proposition: the condition for survival is land reform, the revitalization of the smaller communities of America, and the sharing of all servile tasks. Here it may be that we are the victims of our terminology. "City" is almost inevitably thought of in terms of its prototypes—New York, Chicago, Los Angeles. When we say "the problems of the city" or "urban problems" we hardly ever mean El Centro, California, or Webster City, Iowa, or Dillon, Montana. As we have noted by differentiating "town" from "city," we summon up for the town a mental image of cultural aridity and economic marginality and for the city one of wealth and culture. Perhaps we need another word, a word that indicates *civilized community life* not implying a specific scale. Why not a flourishing "city" of 5,000 as well as a city of 8,000,000? If we could thereby redirect our thinking, we should be able to include in the notion of "city" its countryside, its farms and woodlands, not exploited dependencies, but essential parts of the urbs. We cannot dismantle the huge agencies of exploitation—public and private—in the abstract name of the goodness of smallness, but only in terms of a broader and better vision of our common social life. That and, of course, greater efficiency.

To some, these speculations may seem Utopian. But Utopias can serve a vital need by inducing us to look with new eyes at the status quo that holds our imaginations in thrall. Only by such encompassing formulations can we bring the problems of the urban ghetto, the diminished rural scene, and the dying community together. They are not separate issues; they are all a single issue—the revival of the land and of the people who occupy it. We do not ourselves accept the label "Utopian" because we see all around us the stirrings of a new consciousness and a new determination to restore our society. These new stirrings are given force and focus by the coincidence of the two-hundredth anniversary of the Revolution that established this nation, which we begin to celebrate on December 16th in memory of the Boston Tea Party.

DECENTRALIZATION

It is clear that in almost every segment of the dominant culture there is terrible waste and inefficiency. The truth is that American economic success has made possible inefficiency on a colossal scale. We must remember that until quite recently most work on which an economic value was placed was done at home—farming, most notably, but many "cottage industries" as well. Storekeepers lived in their stores, as did artisans; teachers, not infrequently, taught in their own homes. The industrial revolution and the urbanization of our society changed all that. People began to *go* to work. The collection and organization of large numbers of people in a single location, typically to operate large and costly machines, was the hallmark of the new age. But even at the beginning some enlightened industrialists fought against the tide. The neat apartments, the cultural activities, the good health and spirits of the Lowell, Massachusetts, factory girls were the wonder of the world. But the Lowell factory girls were soon replaced by cheap immigrant labor living in fetid company towns. Following the heyday of the company town, we experienced the intricate social process that we are familiar with today whereby the worker and his work became more and more widely separated, as the city became increasingly uninhabitable and more people were willing to pay a premium in time, energy, and money, to live at a considerable distance from their work—to live in the "sub-urbs" gradually encircling our large cities.

The practice of collecting people together in factories in the name of increased efficiency was imitated by every kind of commercial venture. Even where the use of complicated machines did not dictate the assembling of people in one particular location, it was assumed that this was a more efficient mode of operation, and thus many, many people who did jobs that they could have done as well or better at home or in small shops studied things under supervision and in company with their fellow workers. To "go off to work" became the accepted practice, the standard way of earning a living for most Americans.

But we have long since passed the point of diminishing returns in this mindless process of centralization. We now pay a staggering price for the inefficiency of this American way of life, now known as the "energy crisis." Where the question once was "How can we bring large numbers of people together and organize their work in such a way as to produce a maximum of efficiency?" it is now the reverse: "How can we break up these large, unmanageable, inefficient, and inhuman units into smaller ones?" Whether we look at high schools and universities, industries, hospitals, governmental agencies—whatever—the problems are essentially the same. They are too big, too expensive, and too destructive of people, and often of the environment as well. Some units will doubtless prove not susceptible of decentralization, but the burden of proof should be on them.

For the first hundred years the story of the expansion and development of America was a story of the proliferation of small communities—thousands upon thousands of them stretching all across the United States. Each of these communities felt important, an essential part of the totality that was America. God cared as much for them as he did for the residents of the richest and most powerful urban centers—more, indeed, because these towns considered themselves the purest vessels of the American spirit; they nourished the spirit of hardihood, of piety, of community in all the vast interior regions of America.

In the next hundred years this was reversed. The town—the small community—saw its best human material go, generation after generation, to the city. From having been the vanguard, the true vessel of the spirit, it became a backwater. Power, wealth, culture, and "importance" passed from the town to the great metropolitan centers. The towns became satellites of the great cities, country cousins, looked down on and condescended to. In the recent film *American Graffiti*, the most promising boy in the town, of course, is the one who goes off to college in the East. The town not only accepts this but is proud of it and feels validated by it. The film underlines the small community's loss of potency and authenticity. The town tacitly accepted the notion that all the really important things go on in the great metropolitan centers.

Much of what is most deeply wrong about American life has to do with the fact that small communities have, for almost a hundred years, been drained of their most able and energetic individuals. Meanwhile huge urban centers have become increasingly uninhabitable—crime, smog, drug-taking, neurosis, noise, hideous inconvenience, soul-destroying filth. The big-city cop becomes the hero of television as we become powerless to cope with our cities—to reform them or escape them. All who can afford it live in the suburbs and exhaust themselves traveling to and fro. The cities are, to put the matter simply and directly, appallingly inefficient. Everything is more difficult, more expensive, more exhausting in the city. But we are unable to think in any other terms. Cities dominate our lives and our culture because, however we may yearn for bucolic bliss, we simply cannot imagine living in small communities. In our hearts we believe that all the hideous inconveniences of the city are better endured than the intellectual and cultural barrenness of small communities. And, of course, as long as we believe this it will probably be so, although there are hopeful signs of a cultural renaissance of the small town.

Our tired brains can contain only two alternatives: the feverish, unmanageable city, or the unspoiled countryside. The latter is not an option as it is no longer unspoiled, and the plight of the small farmer trying to make a living and failing is an American tragedy.

Recently in a literary journal, as perceptive a critic as George Steiner took the critics of the city to task as sentimentalists and romantics. While admitting that cities were in more or less desperate straits, he recounted the role of cities in civilization and argued that, unpleasant as the modern city was, we really had no alternative. In so arguing he demonstrated that his own imagination was severely limited and his historical survey faulty. Some of the greatest "cities" of the past, especially those of ancient Greece and Renaissance Italy, were no bigger than large towns. Florence, Venice, Siena, Verona, Padua were towns in terms of present-day urban populations—their "civic humanism" was an expression of their vitality and not their numbers. In other words, there is reason to believe that cultural and intellectual life of great power is possible in communities where it is still possible to live a decent life in simple physical terms.

We believe the most important task in the reconstruction of American society may well be to revitalize the towns. No, to do more than that. To make the towns flower and blossom as the great Renaissance towns of Italy once did and to make them do so in conjunction with the rural land around them. Of course, even if we wished to do away with the huge cities, we could not as they are undoubtedly essential to an industrialized technological society. But by revitalizing the smaller communities of America we would restore a social and economic balance absolutely vital to our health and happiness as a people. This is a gigantic undertaking but at the same time a consolingly simple one. It does not require enormous federal grants, huge bureaucracies, stultifying plans; it only requires a change of heart (the Greek word is *metanoia*—to go beyond your mind and begin again at rock-bottom). It could be accomplished in a decade. Perhaps it is already being accomplished right under our very noses, already summoning our support and active participation.

LAND REFORM

The William James Association is strongly committed to the principle of Land Reform and has taken part in the growing Land Reform Movement in the United States. Certainly the questions raised by the phrase "Land Reform" are many. Is Land Reform simply growing organic vegetables and flowers at a loss? How central to the notion of Land Reform is organic agriculture? In underdeveloped countries, Land Reform has meant, typically, breaking up huge land holdings of wealthy individuals and redistributing the land to landless peasants who were exploited as tenants of the landowners, exemplied by Vinoba Bhave, the successor of Gandhi and the leader of the Land Reform movement in India. In the United States, many farmers in the past four decades have left the land readily and voluntarily for better-paying city jobs. Many others have been forced off by the pressure created by so-called agribusiness, by large agricultural enterprises commanding huge capital and employing advanced agricultural technology with which the small farmer is unable to cope. The result has been a replication in agriculture of that vastness of scale that is so destructive in other segments of society. Nor is the problem confined to farming per se: it spills over into lumber and mining as well. A dozen paper companies own *half* the land in Maine. Pittson Coal Company, having strip-mined West Virginia into the Buffalo Creek flood disaster, is now trying to build a refinery on the Maine Coast (out of 3,500 miles of Maine Coast, only about one hundred are open to the public.)

In the South, in an area as large as Georgia, Alabama, and Mississippi combined, lumber and paper companies pollute the air and water in the process of making paper. In 1910, black farmers in the South owned fifteen million acres; now they own only 5.5 million acres. The story is the same throughout the fifty states. Everywhere corporate farms with much larger capital resources than those available to even the prosperous individual farmer are buying up huge allotments of land, mechanizing their operations to an unprecedented degree, and putting the small farmer at a competitive disadvantage. Ralph Nader found that in California the ten largest landowners in the state owned 12 percent of all the privately owned land.

Everywhere the story is the same—exploitative use of the land by agribusiness, by hit-and-run developers, by lumber companies and mining companies that devastate the landscape and leave it in ruins. It is clear enough that the relation of people to the land they live on and the air they breathe is one of the most crucial issues of our time. The restoration of the land is essential for the restoration of society; we can talk about it because so many young people have invested their lives in the issue. Because they have invested their lives, we have to talk about it!

The land issue, as with the city, huge industry, and the octopus-like conglomerate, is in essence an issue of *bigness*.

Bigness, as the Founding Fathers constantly reiterated, is the occasion, the opportunity, the ground for tyranny and exploitation. In the words of Rosenstock-Huessy, "The fertility of goodness, the contagion of enthusiasm, the fecundity of thought, the influence of authority are interhuman processes which spring to life only between people." They do not spring to life between governmental agencies, between bureaucracies, or between institutions. The more extensive bureaucratic structures become, the more they become remote, abstract, "organized," and rationalized—what Max Weber called "the routinization of the charisma"; and the more they become devoid of spirit, or filled with the spirit of "dead works," as well as corrupt, brutal, and manipulative. This is what we are witnessing in the present administration and all its corporate satellites. Such corruption would not have surprised the Founding Fathers and it should not surprise us if we accept the notion that man has elements of destructiveness in him that are only held in check by "link-work," by, most typically, participation in genuine communities.

It is pointless to declaim about the decline of morality in America and the need for laws to prevent governmental and corporate wrongdoing. The origin of the wrongdoing is quite simply in the scale, in the multiplication of the element of original sin in all of us, and the placing of that multiplied inherent sinfulness, that stigma of finitude, outside any kind of constraining human order. The exploitative impulse is always present and will always outwit the laws designed to contain it when it wields sufficient power to do so. And it will do this in socialist and communist regimes as well as in capitalist ones—probably more successfully in the former since huge governmental bureaucracies will be meshed with huge industrial bureaucracies, although Mao's Cultural Revolution of the Red Guard could be viewed as an internal critical attack on rigidified bureaucracy. At least one suspects that this was partly what the Chinese Cultural Revolution was about—the rapid and threatening growth of the state bureaucracies. The whole Watergate-related scandal underlines this tendency for the governmental and corporate bureaucracies to merge their interests at the cost of the people in general. One might even argue that they are forced to do so to ensure their mutual survival, for their capacity to mortally wound each other is so great that the pressure to conspire is almost irresistible. It was Hannah Arendt who first called attention to this cycle of "the banality of evil" within the climate of the obtuse bureaucrat when she drew her portrait of *Eichmann in Jerusalem*.

Perhaps it is appropriate to quote a passage of William James, which we received from the mouth of Dorothy Day as her favorite Jamesian quote. Transmitted through her spirit, it carries the ring of truth: "As for me, my bed is made: I am against Bigness and Greatness in all their forms, and *with* the invisible molecular moral forces that work from individual to individual, stealing in through the crannies of the world like so many soft rootlets ... rending the hardest monuments of man's pride, if you give them time. The bigger the unit you deal with, the hollower, the more brutal, the more mendacious is the life displayed."

Although it is in the area of Land Reform that federal legislation is most needed and most appropriate, it is here that it is probably the most difficult to get. Congress is much readier to vote some billions of dollars for a program for the urban poor to be administered by thousands of bureaucrats than to restrain the rapacity of lumber companies, strip miners, and other corporate despoilers of the land. This is primarily because in the United States private property is a sacred cow of extraordinary veneration. What most Americans fail to face up to is that the incantation of private property is the cover for the selfish and ruthless exploitation of the American people and the land they live on. This is why the problem of proper income distribution must be the consequence of a genuine reconstruction of our society rather than the means of achieving it.

Legislative means should be found for closing tax loopholes that make it profitable for corporations to invest in land, a tax on the rise in land values, and a progressive property tax, to go with the progressive income tax. States and counties can limit the amount of land owned by an individual or corporation; they can develop tax structures that encourage the small farmer to keep his land in production. Land trusts can acquire land to be worked by individual farmers, by cooperatives, and by community development organizations.

If all this had to be done simply in the name of efficiency and in the face of general public apathy or disinterest, or if it had to be done by the federal government alone, the prospects would be pretty bleak, but the fact of the matter is that the spirit and temper of the people as a whole and of young people in particular seems to be sympathetic to such a "resettlement of America." It may well be that the major task in the re-settling of America is simply that of removing impediments and the principal impediment is doubtless in the way we think: a kind of paralysis of the imagination produced by the power of *isness*, the ubiquity of the existing situation, the mind-dulling reality of the dominating megalopolis.

Our discussions, for example, of the problem of income distribution in the United States revolve almost exclusively around the question of tax reform. But the fundamental issue is not how the government can best take away money from the rich and give it to the poor; the fundamental question is how can people live decent lives? How can society be restructured so that money is not the central and overriding issue?

An important segment of our society—the middle-class young—are already performing remarkable experiments in this regard. The point is not that few, if any, communes are self-supporting—most have to have some kind of supplementary income. The point is that hundreds of thousands of these young people have been willing to live in communes of various kinds in conditions of self-imposed poverty and by doing so have made it prospectively possible for all Americans to free themselves from the cash nexus. The lesson they are trying to teach America is a very simple one indeed: "money isn't everything!" And of course it is not just in communes that the youth of the subculture have demonstrated their disregard for the bitch-goddess Success. Many more not actually living in communes have chosen to live economically marginal lives. Again, like their friends and companions in the communes, they enable us to think in new ways about how to live.